EN GAR
Reflections of rur

Katrina

with good wishes

love

Sandy &
Alistair

EN GARD

Reflections of rural France

ALISTAIR SCOTT
&
SANDY THOMPSON

Leonie Press

ISBN
1 901253 47 3
First published March 2005

© Alistair Scott & Sandy Thompson 2005

The moral right of Alistair Scott and Sandy Thompson to be identified as the authors of this work has been asserted by them in accordance with the Copyright, Designs and Patents Act 1988.

All rights reserved. No part of this publication may be reproduced, stored in a retrieval system, or transmitted in any form or by any means, electronic, mechanical, photocopying, recording or otherwise, without the prior permission of the copyright owner.

Published by:
Léonie Press
an imprint of
Anne Loader Publications
13 Vale Road, Hartford,
Northwich, Cheshire CW8 1PL Gt Britain
Tel: 01606 75660   Fax: 01606 77609
e-mail: anne@leoniepress.com
Website: www.anneloaderpublications.co.uk
www.leoniepress.com

Design and layout by: Anne Loader Publications
Covers laminated by: The Finishing Touch, St Helens
Printed by: MRT @3D www.mrtresponse.com

Alistair Scott and Sandy Thompson

ABOUT THE AUTHORS

LIKE MANY art school graduates **Sandy** had to earn her living doing something completely different for most of her life – working in a casino with a lot of other delightful misfits. She kept the creative flame flickering by writing short stories, making silver jewellery and painting in watercolour.

Moving to France has given her the time and space to write more, and she will be teaching watercolour there, when the dust settles.

Moving to France is the latest adventure for **Alistair**. One amongst many.

Expert at nothing and living in a world of specialists, he's at a slight angle to the rest of the universe, and has turned his hand to many things. Sailor, lecturer, roofer, writer – all part of a rich tapestry. In this small French corner of the universe, he at last feels perfectly at peace.

CONTENTS

Acknowledgements	viii
Dedication	ix
The storm before the calm	1
That's it!!!	2
The first Grand Tour	6
Down to business	10
Warts and all	15
The second visit	19
Second thoughts	24
The third visit and the bid	27
The contract to buy	32
Between exchange and completion	35
The Acte de Vente	41
Give me back my gandmother's wardrobe!	47
May 2002 – Turning on the tap	55
The sisters-in-laws' rabbit stew	58
Surreal soirée	60
A roof over our heads	65
The work crew arrives	68
A weekend at the races	73
Café moments	77
A hat-trick of roofs	82
Madame Bernard's soup	84
Of rats and men	91
November 22nd, 2002 – Road Rage	96
Deux petits canards – 22	99
April 8th, 2003 – Wild food & April fish	103
Paella party	106
Flushing out some local history	115
Ugly rumours	123
Toad in the hole	127

June 2003 – Life is just a jar of cherries	*131*
Payment by pheasant	133
St Lydia's Day, Aug 2003	*138*
Lisette's tomato salad	141
October 19th, 2003 – Harvest moon and howling dogs...	*143*
Fiasco de foie gras	146
A rite of passage	153
Pigs by moonlight	159
March 26th, 2004 – Windswept and waiting for the swallows	*165*
Finding our spot	168
The Aliens are coming	172
Sandy's sixty cloves of garlic with chicken	177
The party to end all parties	179
The end of the beginning	187
Sketch plan of the house	188

ACKNOWLEDGEMENTS

We would like to thank Ian, Ann and Joanne Scott for their ceaseless enthusiasm for the house and the book. Everything would have been harder without them, their hard work and support. The Thompsons, Keith and Lesley, did their bit too, between bites of cheese.

To Denny Davis-Taylor, who, from 4000 miles away, kept our spirits up when the going got tough.

To Sue Cowell, Jean and Dick Parsons, Lynda Field, to Denny again, and everyone who wrote good old-fashioned letters – they were always a joy to receive in this age of e-mail.

We are indebted to Damien and Lisa @ Cybercafe Jourdan Informatique in Uzès, under whose patient guidance the book made it from longhand on foolscap to CD. And thanks for all the chocolate biscuits too.

To Anne and Jack Loader at Léonie Press, the friendly face of publishing.

Finally, thanks to our village, who welcomed us into their midst and made our house our home.

Alistair Scott
Sandy Thompson
February 2005

DEDICATION

This book is dedicated to our parents, with thanks for the genes of humour, hard work and bloody-mindedness – but especially to Pooh, who never got to sit in the courtyard with her crosswords, and to The Duchess, who may yet be tempted, by the patisserie, to visit.

AS & ST

THE STORM BEFORE THE CALM

SAILING, we knew two storms.

The first was a squall, a fairground-ride of a storm. It came upon us fast. Thunder-head clouds on the horizon – anvils in the sky. A rapid dip in temperature. Unearthly stillness. Lightning that was a release. Hail or rain with enough substance to flatten the ocean to glass, and then a belting wind. Awesome for a few seconds and then it was gone. Sunshine followed and a "what the hell was that?" Laughter, a hot drink, and put some sails back up.

The other was an older storm, longer travelled and altogether slower. Malevolent. It built and built over hours. We could smell it. It darkened everything in its path. It cowed long before it battered. It teased, while the glass fell too far for any good to come of it. Then it magnified. We could lie a-hull, give to its strength, like long grass; drip oil onto the water to quell the frenzy; run before it – away from it, if you like; pray to something bigger. The praying didn't stop the damage. The boat was fine but our strength, our spirit and our resolve took a hammering. The storm lasted a long time, and we came away from it changed.

There has been one other storm. Ashore. In Brighton. Slow to become apparent. Changing our environment beyond recognition, testing us to destruction, hurting us, making us sure we have no place here. We have bobbed like a cork to avoid its savagery; we have fought it; we trimmed everything to weather it better. We have made our incantations to all the powers, but now it is time to run before it. We shall harness its energy and make for France.

THAT'S IT!!!

A TURBOCHARGER had kicked into our hunt for a home in France. The monthly dose of subscription magazines, and the occasional response from an estate agent, were no longer fuel enough for us. We needed the internet. That took some swallowing, given that by nature, we both have something of the Luddite about us.

Eventually there were two or three sites we trusted, and visited time and again. On a Christmas trip to Yorkshire we had the use of my brother's computer and went straight to work with 'Latitudes.com.' We typed in our usual requirements, "a village house in stone, under £60,000, in need of restoration". This time they linked us to an *immobilier* in a town we didn't know, in an area we'd never considered. An image formed on the screen, starting with the sky, an eye-blue sky, followed by a roof of curved tiles in earthy colours, two arches and a terrace, outside stone steps (always a must for Sandy), and a third larger arch – making-up a child's face of a facade. A large courtyard, enclosed on three sides by the house and outbuildings, with rusty, but imposing, iron gates. The whole absorbed the bright sunshine and emitted a pink glow from stone and rendering.

Sandy, slow and thoughtful in most ways, fell in love with the place as the image unfolded. She simply said, "That's it."

Above the photo there was a reference number and a vague location, which meant nothing to us – Ales/Bagnols, Gard. Alongside the image was the scant information that was to beguile most of our waking hours for the next nine months. "Character village house with a 300m$_2$ interior courtyard and the possibility of obtaining some land. Situated in the Gard between Ales & Bagnols. 200m$_2$ of living space in need of renovation, 60m$_2$ of outbuildings, garage, 3 beautiful vaulted cellars, covered terrace."

Printing off the image was beyond our skills, and we had to

THAT'S IT!!!

wait for the evening and help from my brother. At A4 we could see fig saplings growing out of the walls, brambles chest-high in the courtyard, and all the gaps in the roof tiles. It was beautiful. We asked for more details.

Travelling back to Brighton a few days later, we stopped off in London to visit a French Property Exhibition.

I know a lot of people don't believe in coincidence or Fate. But, coincidentally and Fatefully, the first stand as we entered the hall was 'Latitudes'. Dead centre, on a notice-board, at exactly our eye level, radiating its pink glow, was the house we'd printed off in Yorkshire. A sharp intake of breath from Sandy, "Scotty, it's here!"

I couldn't speak. Every hair on my body was standing on end. Strange forces were at work.. It was like looking at cave paintings while listening to whale music. The house worked its magic on me, as it had on Sandy. I tried and tried to look at photos of other houses, but I couldn't do it. Too much like having Pirelli calendars around the bedroom on your wedding night, disloyal and irrelevant.

Pulling myself together I went into the 'Latitudes' stand, hoping to get more details. They were busy. When we were finally handed the details of the pink house, they were exactly as before. No nitty gritty. We were hungry for information about its age and history, about the village and the area.

"Don't you know anything more about the property?" I asked. The young woman took the single page, read and handed it back to me. "No, this is all we have. But I do know, at this price, it won't be all of that." She pointed to the photo. "Not so close to Uzès. It's probably divided up." And she was whisked away by another client.

"That can't be right," said Sandy "Look at all those square metres. It must be the whole house." We felt flattened. There was an unspoken "now what?" in our mood. We made a half-hearted and distracted tour of the other stands, picked up a few more brochures and bits of paper, comforted ourselves with some good food and wine.

"And who or what is 'Uzès' anyway?" I asked.

"If we want more information we'll have to find out for ourselves; get some guide books tomorrow."

We took big strides the next day. A high quality road atlas of France, and some Rough Guides to southern 'departments' and a Cadogan guide with plenty of history and background for us to read and digest. Days later we had a response from Eurofoncier to our Yorkshire e-mail. Same sheet of information, slightly larger photo. We began to imagine that the reticence to tell us more might have a sinister motive. Was there a pig farm next door? A nuclear power station at the end of the street? Were there plans for a motorway past the gates? Had it been used in chemical or biological experiments? We needed to go and see for ourselves.

It was January and, with work pressures and lack of holiday time, it would be September before we made the trip. In the meantime we had to hope that the French property market didn't catch fire, and that no-one else bought the house.

For the spring and summer months, our dreams and plans would keep us awake or send us to sleep. They would enchant and unsettle us, and insidiously took over our lives.

Drunk one night in my local pub, I came clean amongst acquaintances I knew through the bottom of a pint glass, about moving to France – and about selling our Brighton house, with its unfinished kitchen.

By closing time, bellies distended with real ale, and with the rash promise of free holidays for life in the south of France, a pair of jobbing builders had agreed to finish the kitchen. As long as they had no other work to do, they would muck in and do the clever stuff, if I did the preparation. The kitchen had been a project that ran out of steam and money. We had muddled through for years without cupboards and surfaces, but when it came to selling the house, it was a definite eyesore. It was never going to be beautiful, but it had to be recognisable as a kitchen at least.

I woke knowing that plans made with pints in hand had counted for little in my life. But those two, drunk or sober, were as good as their word. The kitchen got its makeover. They never really knew how pivotal they were to getting things off the ground – and they never asked for a penny. The offer of a holiday still stands.

Having found a work crew in the local pub, I wondered if I

THAT'S IT!!!

might find a buyer for the house there too.

"Evening. Pint of Harvey's please. I'm selling my house."

"How much?" said the woman at the table behind me.

I told her and added, "I think it's worth more."

"St Martins Place is it – not St Martins Street?"

"That's right."

"I'll buy it – if I can see it tomorrow and if I can get the mortgage."

She saw it and she arranged the mortgage. As simply as that the house was sold, and things got very serious, very quickly.

Eight weeks later, goods and chattels in storage, we set out to buy a campervan. A home between houses, and an alternative to hotel bills or renting gites. A vehicle which would give us a way to criss-cross France with freedom. And finally a dormitory should we need one, while making a house – hopefully the pink house – habitable.

THE FIRST GRAND TOUR

IN SEPTEMBER we bought the cheapest ferry ticket we could find, for ourselves and 'Blue', as the camper had become known.

Sandy the Navigator had planned a route south with two things in mind. Firstly, that we took in as many places as possible which, at one time or another, had had property that interested us. It would be a chance to see if imagination and reality overlapped at all. Secondly, perhaps more importantly, the route was to be as kind as possible to 'Blue'. She was not at her best on long steep inclines, and there were plenty of those between us and our destination. The motorways had a crawl lane for HGV traffic, and we would have to use it too. On smaller hilly roads everything had to slow to our 50kph – and this in a country where great-grandmothers like to put their foot down. We knew we would get there, but never quickly, laden as we were with everything including a kitchen sink. As we went up the steeper stretches we would sing Thomas the Tank Engine's song, "I-think-I-can, I-think-I-can", and as we reached the top, "I-know-I-can, I-know-I-can", to keep our spirits high.

On the evening of our first day, adrenaline dried up outside Le Mans. I dreamt of day-long races and cars that could accelerate. In the morning we had a Full French Breakfast, *croissants au beurre* and gallons of coffee strong enough to set our hearts pounding and our hands shaking.

South on the N138 past Tours and Limoges, and already the light was changing. Slate and grey gave way to rich earthy colours. Farmscapes had other crops and other cattle. Horizons were lengthening, space was opening up. We were halfway there.

It was a heady time. Sights, smells and tastes were different; a meteorite storm of difference. We were enjoying a wonderful sense of freedom. If there was a pretty riverside, we could make it our lunch stop. Our night-camp could be chosen for its view of the

THE FIRST GRAND TOUR

sunset. We liked this travelling life.

On and on south, mocking hatchbacks and sports cars who left us behind in their dust, for not having their own beds and loos. Past Cahors – pronounced with as much phlegm as you can muster – and Rodez and Millau. This was the high country and the going was slow. Just after Millau we were in the right region at last, Languedoc-Rousillon. South of that was the Mediterranean.. Lamalou-les-Bains was going to be our night stop. We'd had a lot of responses from the estate agents there, with old stone houses within our budget, and we were curious.

We knew it was a spa town; its waters highly regarded for hundreds of years by French doctors. Clearly, soaking and washing away ailments had been a lucrative business; the main street was lined with mansions from the 'Belle Époque', now fallen on hard times and into disrepair. We might have been reminded of Bath or Harrogate, if not for the population out and about in the streets. It was as if a large local hospital had been evacuated and the patients left to wander aimlessly, waiting for the 'all clear'. It is a strange feeling to be able-bodied, in a town where 90% of the residents are incapacitated and the other 10% are caring for them. Pavements filled with ambulatory patients pushing the wheelchairs of less able friends; so many that a traffic scheme was in operation. In restaurants, those who could feed themselves also fed those who could not. Limbs were dressed and bandaged; necks were artificially supported and there was a faint odour of ointment, surgical spirit and decay. Every now and then, a visiting relative stood out from the crowd, rosy-cheeked and smart, amid the pallid and scaly in dressing-gowns and slippers. Conversations compared maladies and treatments, large amounts of time were spent making people comfortable.

It was obvious why the old stone houses were so cheap. We ate and slept and made plans to get down to the coast next day, to Cap D'Agde, for a swim in the late autumn sunshine.

I must go down to the sea again...

The Mediterranean had long before taken on a special significance for me. Its cultures at various times formed our modern world – philosophically, theologically, politically. Its citizens had advanced us scientifically; their art and technology the basis of so much we take for granted today. Quantum leaps in civilisation happened around its shores. I'd taken a quantum leap here too – into an absurd notion of adulthood.

On holiday, as a young man, I walked from my rented fisherman's cottage, drank a small bottle of champagne and orange juice, and swam in the sea on the French-Spanish Mediterranean border. During the swim I floated on my back, lowered my trunks and urinated. As I watched the stream of urine arc against a pure blue sky and patter into the water, I had said out loud "This is it. This is the life."

Thirty years later I was here to pee again; a bit further along the coast, a bit further along my life. There was still some angst, and plenty of drive, but I was mellower. There is some virtue in growing older.

In my relative calm, floating in the warm waters off Cap D'Agde, I looked over the sea and up at the sky. It was as if I'd never really thought about blue before. I knew it as a woman's eyes or a mother's hat, school ties and butterflies; but this was overwhelming colour, rich and uninterrupted. I wondered if I needed to call it blue-blue; to distinguish it from all the excuses for blue I'd known before. Lapis lazuli, cobalt and woad paled in comparison. It was a blue that flooded the senses.

My Scottish Presbyterian father would try and nullify colour by surrounding it with something bland; bright ties and grey suits. He took a big risk buying a bottle-green car. Colour was the work of the Devil, and had to be subdued.

Here it seemed there was a different attitude to colour; to blue-blue. Don't mute or camouflage or cover it; add to it. Add red and yellow, and mix them. Add oranges and lemons and olives in the trees, and lavender in the fields. Combinations and variations of all of them on anything that moves – summer dresses, fluttering tablecloths and parasols; on iron gates and shutters; around necks and on ears, on every flat and vertical surface. Then wait for those with a seriously keen eye to come and record it. Matisse, Picasso, Cezanne and Van Gogh are the names we all know, but a thousand others did it too. Transported by the intensity and clarity of colour

THE FIRST GRAND TOUR

they came to paint it large. When you tire of the natural world, a bowl of *bouillabaisse* or plate of *paella* offers the same profusion, but edible. And there is the rosé, our first taste of Côtes du Rhône wine; delicate and daintily pink. Slightly drunk, we decide that no one would believe the colours in the sunset, even in a photograph, and that sunsets are best left in the sky, where they belong.

We head for another 'Blue', the van. With three days left before we can visit the pink house, legitimately, we make some subversive plans to find her ourselves.

DOWN TO BUSINESS

JOINING THE A9 north of Cap D'Agde, turn left to be in Barcelona for supper, or like us, turn right towards Montpellier and Nîmes. Follow signs to Orange; even place-names hereabouts get your mouth watering. Away from the sea and the coastal plain, parched in late summer, and into an ocean of green scrubland, the *garrigue*. We pass *'aires'*, offering oysters or an archaeological site or a giant sundial, to entertain you when you need a break from driving. Taking the exit for Bagnols-sur-Cèze, we are both overcome by a sense of being at home. Not *'déjà vu'*, certainly not familiarity; hard to explain to ourselves or each other, impossible to anyone else.

Bagnols was to be our base for the visit; our starting point for 'casing the joint' as the villains say in old movies. But we had two pressing needs to meet at once. A place to park 'Blue', safe and quiet enough to sleep and then a bar-café with a decent loo, which opened at an hour that suited our requirements. These requirements could be pressing. Our diet had changed from northern European to southern, with its abundance of fresh fruit and vegetables and olive oil. Individually all wonderful laxatives. And together, quite unstoppable. It was a continuation of one of our navigational priorities – avoiding the nightmare Turkish bog. A hole in the cement floor, with foot-shaped impressions either side for squatting. It doesn't matter what you wear, unless it's a flowing djellaba to hoick up around your waist, it will get soaked. They flush copiously and leave big puddles. Public toilets in market squares are guaranteed to be 'squats'. I'm told your aim gets better with practice, but I've seen no evidence of that.

We chose a tree-shaded car park to put the van, and were woken every morning by singing street cleaners. Close by, Le Café d'Industrie provided our toiletry requirements and our breakfast, and became a home from home. It must have been obvious how we were using his establishment, but *Monsieur le patron*, with just a small wink, still treated us like his most valuable paying customers. It is a delightful idea, that a cup of coffee buys you a table in a café, for as long as you want – though etiquette suggests you vacate it for the lunch hour.

Like Baldric, we had a cunning plan. Knowing only that it was somewhere between Bagnols and Ales, Sandy had an idea about using a grid system to search for the house. We wanted to find it, before we met the estate agent, to take a look at the village and the countryside around. The main road between the two towns was 46 kilometres. We were to zigzag across it, up and down hills, along winding country roads, searching left and right looking for the distinctive twin arches. If a village felt promising, we were to get out and walk around. Sandy's idea, she said, was based on archaeological grids; and the archaeologists missed nothing.

Fortified with the infallibility of the plan, we managed to empty the fuel tank three times in two days. We used binoculars, a compass and survey maps. In bright sunshine, we walked around empty hamlets with only a friendly dog for company. On hill-tops and in valleys, no corner was left unrounded, no stone was left unturned. We saw a house with a tree growing through the roof, tumbledown turreted gems behind elaborate iron gates, a geodesic dome in a field of cacti, and hand-painted 'For sale' signs on shepherd's huts and shacks, but we didn't find our arches.

Knowing the estate agent's paranoia of owner and buyer meeting and cutting them out of a deal, we assumed the main Bagnols to Ales road would be the last place to find the house. We stayed off it. Our sorties took us further afield; the grid expanded. Remember, archaeologists miss nothing. Undaunted, we continued the search, without admitting for a second the absolute futility of it. On the evening of the second day, we conceded, without acrimony that we would never make archaeologists; we had missed it. But the plan had occupied us for what otherwise would have been two interminable days of anticipation and frustration. It had served a purpose, and we knew the area much better now. Tomorrow we were going to see the house, by appointment, and we unwound with a pastis.

EN GARD

Early next morning we were woken, before the street cleaners, by thunder and lightning, and rain drumming on the roof of the camper. We waited as long as we could before making the dash to the *immobilier*. We had brought the kitchen sink, but no umbrella. The heavens opened and we arrived for the nine-month-old appointment looking like monsoon rats. The office staff were startled by the sight of us, dripping onto the carpet like a couple of melting ice lollies, or perhaps by our punctuality. We took seats to wait for Madame de la Fuente. She swept in, dry and elegant under a huge golf umbrella, late as required by a thousand years of precedent, but not late enough to be rude or cause inconvenience.

Bespectacled, and with just a smidgen of make-up, she marched towards us, hand extended, with a warm and confident *"Bonjour Monsieur Scott!"* The handshake was firm and lingering, as she took us in from sodden head to toe.

"I know what you most want to see," she said, "but I'd like to suggest that there may be two other houses for you to look at today. If you agree, it also gives me the chance to show you some of the countryside."

Of course we agreed. I knew that, carried along by her confidence and her enthusiasm, I would have trusted anything she suggested. In all the hours we were to spend with her, I was never to feel otherwise. In the months ahead she was always completely in control of events, on top of problems and almost maternal in her solicitude. We were flabbergasted that she felt it was part of her remit to give us a guided tour. No estate agent in Brighton took us down to the beach or around the Pavilion or into the good pubs.

Within the hour we were in a small French car, which, after the trip in 'Blue', seemed to travel at the speed of sound. We headed north of Bagnols towards the Ardèche gorges. Madame de la Fuente drove like a demon. In the short gaps when she was not overtaking, she pointed out good roadside spots to find peaches, cherries and asparagus from local growers. She showed us the *'domaine'* where she bought her white wine, and a *'cave'* for the best red. Here was a good place to canoe, there was a pretty picnic site, and beyond a mushroom wood. She went collecting every weekend in September, she said. One eye on the road, one hand on the wheel, she turned off into the hills.

House number one was fine enough. We wound upwards around hairpin bends through spruce, chestnuts and terraces of apple trees. Coming down the same way in winter might not be much fun. The storm had passed and we were drying out. It was cold and sunny, and very quiet. You could hear a pine cone drop. The village was divided by a small river, crossed by a single-arched bridge. Not a soul on the streets. The house stood end-on to the road; a pair of wooden doors took up most of the lower wall, held closed by a padlock about the size of a frying-pan. We walked down the narrow lane on the left and saw three more pairs of huge wooden doors. Built up-and-over the last pair was a mossy stone staircase. Each tread worn smooth and concave by a hundred years of hungry husbands coming home to eat three times a day. There was a heavy planked door at the top, and Mme de la F. produced an iron key, fit for any dungeon.

Inside there was a rabbit warren of musty rooms, one with a dead kitten, and lots of fallen plaster. A part of the roof was down, and a soggy chestnut beam in two pieces on the floor. There was a courtyard with two shaggy pines, but no direct access from the house. No sun ever warmed its flagstones, which were slimy with bright green moss. Back inside we were shown the vaulted rooms behind those wooden doors, and were dumbstruck by Mme de la F.'s calculation that, in total, there was 500m2 of living and working space. It was a lot of house for the money, but it buttered no parsnips with us. It wasn't where we wanted to be.

House number two took us down the hill, onto a plain of vineyards and into a sleepy village with flowers climbing and hanging from every wall and window-ledge. The house turned out to be fascinating, for the insight it offered into what was really important in life hereabouts. It was in the village square, opposite the church, and had an ornately carved lintel over arched wooden doors. Tall and wide enough for a man on a tractor, the doors were ribbed like corduroy where softer wood tissue had been burnt away by scorching sun and washed away by torrential rain – something like a living fossil. They opened noisily to reveal a

EN GARD

cathedral of a room. A vineyard tractor was parked on the left and there was a path straight ahead, one man wide. The rest of the space was taken up by a stainless steel cylinder, maybe forty feet high and thirty feet in diameter, sunk into the floor. A wrought-iron staircase snaked around it and catwalks circled it. The cement floor was stained dark red and the closed doors had incubated the smells of wine, vinegar and must. If you wanted to go into wine production, to become a *vigneron*, this was the place for you. Outside the heavy old doors, stone steps led to the rest of the house. This was two rooms, a living-room/kitchen and a bedroom/bathroom; 1950s flowery wallpaper, a cracked sink and French windows onto a rickety balcony. That was it. The occupants had put up with cramped and spartan conditions, and devoted themselves to what mattered more than creature comforts – the production of good red wine.

Madame de la Fuente with some foxiness and professional licence, had saved the best till last. We were impatient now to see the pink house. En route she took a lengthy detour to show us the Ardèche gorges where we paused for a photo shoot and a cigarette. The view was magnificent, the delay an agony, the tobacco welcome. Back onto main roads, past a good spot for watermelons and another for artichokes, and I began to recognise places and names that had been on Sandy's grid. We must be getting close. Just off the Bagnol/Ales road, into a higgledy-piggledy village, past the Mairie, the clocktower and *boulangerie*, down a street one car wide, overhung with wisteria, and she skidded to a stop on the gravelly road.

"*Eh voilà!*" said Mme de la F. and she got out. Sandy got out too. I stayed where I was, staring straight ahead, aware of the house in the corner of my eye. I realised we had missed it in our grid search by about a hundred yards. Turning my head to the right now was going to change my life, and I girded my loins.

WARTS AND ALL

IT'S A SOBERING thought, but psychologists say we make up our minds about people within ten seconds of meeting them. Gut feelings, they're often called; born of subconscious preferences for shapes of noses, the space between eyes, angles of mouths, an expression, a posture – all in ten seconds.

If it's true of people, then, in our case anyway, it's true of houses. This one was better in the flesh, warts and all. She was neglected and abandoned – a calendar for 1982 in a room, suggesting it was at least twenty years since anyone had paid her much attention. But, like a woman with beautiful bone structure, she was lovely behind the brambles, lichen and swifts' nests hanging from every light fitting. The colour of the walls was changing as clouds came and went, from pink to milky coffee; the stone beneath the patchy rendering a mixture of granite and sandstone. Arranged in a horseshoe around a courtyard of feral figs, elderberries, nettles and the vicious brambles, she had evolved over generations, through fortunes good and bad. In the way of most farms, until recent times, animals had lived on part of the ground floor, and the family above. The difference marked in this house, by beautiful tiles or cobbles, by plastered or bare stone walls. An outside stone staircase led up to a covered terrace, from which, through the twin arches, a view of hills and fields of sunflowers could be had. Madame de la Fuente perched herself in one of these arches, to enjoy some sun and a smoke. She waved her hand, "Take all the time you want," and closed her eyes peacefully.

Where to begin? Upstairs and downstairs there were no corridors; rooms led one into another, up a step here, down two steps there. On the ground floor, in what had been the kitchen, now full of autumn leaves, there was a stone fireplace big enough to roast an ox. From the vaulted ceiling, along with the swifts' nests, hung iron hooks for hams and home-made sausage. Through the next vaulted room with wall-cupboards of wormy wood, into an icy cold room with more hooks in the ceiling and wooden stalls for hay. Turning to the right, two more rooms with chutes in their ceilings for feeding down the hay into more wooden stalls. Back the way we'd come, out and up the staircase to the terrace. Mme de la F opened one eye and smiled *"ça va?"* and went back to her sun-bathing. Through one door, turn right into a high-ceilinged room with a stone arch, or turn left into two tiled rooms full of family rubbish – rotten picture frames, an old highchair, sacks of musty clothes; the window in the end room would open onto sunsets. Up a flight of stone steps and into two attics above the tiled rooms. A good look at the main roof timbers didn't fill me with dread. From the terrace another door, really just a hole in the wall, led to two tall rooms with stoned-up windows. Mystery rooms; no animal ever lived here, but surely no people either? Mme de la F. stretched her legs and came to tell us of an ancient window tax, when the frugal or miserly had filled in unnecessary windows. The second of these rooms led out onto a flat roof; the room below described as a 'garage', to which apparently there was no key...

Retracing our steps we went down into the brambles. An outbuilding on the west side of the courtyard, and running the length of it – fourteen giant strides we measured – was accessible by a creaky metal door. Inside desiccated old sheepshit was knee-high and everything was held together with rusty wire. There was a spectacular arch halfway along, and beyond that warped barn-doors were letting in rays of sunlight.

"This is my studio," whispered Sandy.

Not, you notice, might be or could be. No, this IS my studio; this is MY studio.

Originally there had been another arch under the terrace, but this was partially stoned-in to create two odd rooms, with Fred Flintstone windows covered with chicken-wire. Pigs? Poultry? More mystery.

All this time we had been taking photographs, doubting our ability to remember it all later. With a last longing look around, we called up to Mme de la F., our imaginations fired and our heads buzzing, and we all headed back to Bagnols, to eat, drink and talk

WARTS AND ALL

about 'our' house.

Trying to reconstitute the house and reproduce our tour of it wasn't easy. I was hopeless. Doors and windows and whole rooms were on the move. If I was convinced something was on the ground floor, Sandy was certain it was not; rooms I thought had windows, Sandy was sure had none. Two things worked against me; firstly, a kind of 'museum tour fatigue'. I have looked at everything closely, but remember nothing clearly; saturated by images and information, my brain shuts down to prevent overload. Secondly, the house fell outside any frame of reference I had.

English houses, great and small, follow a familiar formula. They have halls and landings. Somewhere to cook, somewhere to sit around, somewhere to wash, somewhere to sleep. It's all decided for you. Windows have glass, doors have knobs, and there is one flight of stairs and it's always inside. You can't lose yourself. You can't lose your vacuum cleaner.

The pink house had never been designed. It was a famine and feast house. A growing family, some stepchildren and some grandchildren, a good price for lamb, a bumper crop of pearl barley, were the rhymes and reasons for extensions or refinements. When all the mulberry trees were diseased and died, silk farms went broke and horns were pulled in. Labour would be laid off, more space given over to sheep and goats, whose milk and meat was always marketable. Even when we developed the photographs I doubted if I could identify anything other than the kitchen and the two tiled rooms. I wanted to see the house again. I had to see the house again.

"Madame, thank you for everything today. We think the house is wonderful, but there is too much to take in. We feel we need to make another visit," I said to Mme de la F. She checked her diary and we agreed to meet at the house on Tuesday morning.

"The house is better than we dreamed it would be," I added.

Mme de la F. looked at us very keenly, and with some weight she said, 'The whole world dreams of this house, Monsieur Scott. But the work..."

"You are right about the work, but the house has great possibilities. It will be beautiful when it is finished."

EN GARD

She'd gone out of her way today, in both senses, and we wanted to show we didn't take it for granted. Especially as it must be one of the cheapest houses on the books. We offered some money towards petrol.

"*Non, non.* Very kind, but *non.*" She shook her head, laughed, and was gone.

"Would you like to eat now?" asked Sandy

"Spaghetti. About a kilo, and a bottle of red wine. I want to sleep like a baby tonight."

THE SECOND VISIT

IT ISN'T SURPRISING that Sandy's memories of the first visit and mine were so different. Her eye is tuned to detail; aesthetics govern all. I was preoccupied with the work and the skills involved – I would be doing it after all. We were agreed on a couple of things – that it was a big beautiful house, and, if at all possible, we wanted to spend the rest of our lives there. The disagreements about details and workload might be sorted out by the second visit. We'd specifically look at how bad the roof was, the integrity of stone walls, the jack-of-no-trades wiring looped around like linguini. Neither of us could remember any plumbing; not a single tap.

Impatient to have our personal theories about the layout supported by some photographic evidence, we had three rolls of film expressly developed, for about the cost of a decent lunch. We spread them over a table in Café de l'Industrie, a dozen at a time.

The hundred photos still showed the house to be glorious, but they also laid bare the magnitude of the work to be done. We would have to take our time at the next visit. Make some notes. Ask lots of questions. Until then we had a free weekend, and we wanted to explore.

During that fruitless search for 'our' house, we had covered a lot of ground. But we had been under pressure and it hadn't been a pleasure. On Saturday we took the Bagnols to Ales road with a different perspective and without a bloody grid.

There were long open views, with faraway mountains, like a watercolour exercise in distance – pale, paler, palest blues and greys. In the foreground a rolling ocean of *garrigue*, complete with peaks and troughs. Wild shrubland of gorse and oak and holly, with wild thyme and sage underfoot; buzzards cruising above it and wild boar rooting through it. Huge rivers have cut lazily east-west through the limestone to create the gorges, where you can canoe naked with only the buzzards to see you. Important not to forget that this is wine country and farmland too. In late autumn the sky is full of smoke as fields of sunflower stubble are burnt off. Other fields, of asparagus, have turned old gold, and crumbly fruitcake soil has been ploughed, waiting for next year's melons and tomatoes. Roadside plane trees and the last of the vines are ablaze with red and orange.

Rising out of the *garrigue* are hill-top villages; cool narrow lanes full of cats and washing. Stone houses submerged in geraniums. Wrought-iron bell towers clanging out the hours a few minutes late. Faded courtyard doors, patchwork repaired with one more plank of wood and some nails. Fancy net curtains twitching and radios tuned to philosophy phone-ins. In the larger villages there are weekly markets of local cheeses, fruit and veg – and as winter approaches, the odd stall of long johns, woolly hats and socks. It didn't look as if we were ever going to be bored.

On Tuesday Madame de la Fuente arrived just late enough for us to notice. In our enthusiasm we had arrived an hour early, drinking coffee in the van, taking a few more photos. I felt bound to say that the visit might take some time, and, if she had things to do, she could leave us to it and come back later.

"Take as long as you like, Monsieur Scott. All day if necessary."

Sandy, armed with sketchbook and pen, a torch and a tape measure, fought her way past the guard-brambles and went in through the kitchen door. She was intent on making floor plans and notes, gathering clues about the house's history.

I set off to assess the work, and to wonder what sort of fool would think of undertaking it single-handedly. I started in Sandy's 'studio'. The walls looked sound, no frightening bulges or cracks. Up to four feet thick, they were either solid throughout, or built like a sandwich, with a filling of small stones and mortar between two outer courses. The stones themselves were as small as a child's hand or big enough to embarrass two men in their lifting. The only stone to have been cut and worked was in the lintels and around the door. There was an arch dividing the room, and I thought then as I think now, that they are wonderful shapes as well as engineering masterpieces. The roof, although in a bad state, seemed

THE SECOND VISIT

simple enough; three tree-trunk beams crossed by split branches with interlocking curved tiles sitting between them. The oldest of these tiles would have been made by hand, spreading a rhomboid of clay over the curve of a man's thigh, cutting the clay off with a clean edge and firing it in a charcoal kiln. Months later, when we began to take tiles down, we could recognise in them, left and right, fat and thin thighs. The slope of the roof was critical for laying the tiles, as they weren't pinned or secured in any way.

I can guess my latitude from the pitch of roofs around me, from steep Swiss chalets which shuck off the snow, to the flat roofs of fincas in arid southern Spain. This part of France escapes the worst of Europe's weather. The gentle pitch of the roof allows the tiles to be laid loose, relying on their weight to keep them in place. It's simple, and it has a drawback; a clap of thunder or a wandering cat can dislodge a tile. If water comes in and rots a batten, more tiles slip. With no-one around to push things back in place, more water comes through, and eventually a beam rots. And then the roof collapses. This sequence was well underway in the 'studio'. The whole lot would have to be re-done. Not complicated, but there were some mighty weights involved. Just the sort of job for unskilled optimists who don't mind the smell of Deep Heat.

Opposite the 'studio' was the garage, for which there was still no key. There were two windows with broken shutters, protected by beaten iron bars set into the quoins and lintels, in the shape of headless geckos, their legs curved sharp barbs. I found an old stool, two legs good one leg bad, and some flat stones to build a makeshift viewing platform to look inside. The bars were designed to stop a man putting his head and shoulders above or below or between them. They work. With the help of a torch I could just make out a complex vaulted ceiling and a jumble of badly stacked furniture. The furniture might mean that it was reasonably dry. Then the stool fell over, one leg good two legs bad, turned to dust by worm.

I had come away from the first visit with the firm conviction that the house was almost equally divided; the left side, on both floors, had benefited from human habitation, while the right side had not. If we started on the left, with its fireplaces and tiled

EN GARD

floors, making the roof good, we'd soon have six basically habitable rooms. I could perfect my roofing skills on the 'studio' roof; one storey high and not so far to fall. The right side, with the bare walls and cobbles, could wait; or we could always get some sheep or cattle... We could live in the garage if it was dry, and move into the house later. It felt do-able. I needed to talk to Sandy, and to find out what she'd discovered.

I stomped my way through the bramble thicket towards the door that Sandy had disappeared through, like the rabbit in Alice in Wonderland. Cursing the thorns I promised them that they would be my first job. Stepping into the main house it was immediately cooler, and darker; restful and refreshing coming in from the sunny courtyard, or from a hard day in the fields. Sandy appeared in an inside doorway, cobwebs in her hair.

"Having fun?" I asked "What have you been up to?"

"I've done a floor plan, a rough one, up and downstairs with measurements. Every room is about the same size – 25m2. Have you noticed the windows?"

"There aren't any, you mean?"

"Well, not on the back wall. That's north-facing, so no windows means no draughts when the wind blows. Animals didn't need windows, so none over on that side; and then the tiled rooms have one or two each and their shutters look OK. A couple in the attic, but no glass."

"I need to get up in the attic and do a proper check on that roof."

"Let's go. By the way the tiles in those rooms are *'tres characteristique'* and *'tres cher'* according to Madame, and we're lucky to have them. She came round with me and answered all my questions. I spat in the dust and washed the tiles off a bit – the colours are still bright. And over the kitchen door I found two dates, 1807 and a Napoleonic year 16, whenever that was; Madame couldn't remember, but her husband is a teacher and she'll ask him. I found a really old lintel with 1730 scratched into it, but Madame thinks it may have been taken from a local ruin when they built that room; this house isn't that old."

"I hope you've noticed there's about two acres of re-pointing to

THE SECOND VISIT

do on all these walls," I said.

"I'll do that," Sandy replied. "That's just the sort of mindless job I like."

We arrived in the attics and I started to take stock of the six big beams and the gaps in the tiles.

"I love it up here. Look at all this stuff to sort through." Sandy said.

The floors were littered with pre-war toys and games, tins of letters, sacks of clothes, horse collars and harnesses, and agricultural ironmongery. Her idea of heaven.

"I've taken some more photos," she said.

"Oh good," I smiled, wondering where we'd find a flat surface big enough for the collection.

We'd both done everything we'd come to do, and so we thanked Mme de la F., whose tan had deepened since this morning, and hoped we hadn't spoilt her lunch again. She tutted and said

"Of course not! But next time we will have lunch together."

She locked up, and we asked again about the building without a key. I said I needed to check if it was dry inside.

"I will talk to the owner. Let me know if you decide anything – we can always make another visit," and there was a twinkle in her eye.

"Before we go, Madame," Sandy asked pointing to the village name on a road-sign, 'Why do all the villages around here end in 'argues'? What does it mean?"

"I don't know," said Mme de la F, "I'm not a local."

"You're not?!"

"Oh no, I'm from Lyon. I've only been here 26 years."

SECOND THOUGHTS

"IT CAN'T BE this easy," said Sandy, and I knew exactly what she meant.

When we bought our boat, it was the third one we looked at. When we bought the house in Brighton, it was the third one we saw. And now we were seriously thinking of buying the third house we had seen in France. Were we lucky, focused – or just easy to please? After all the horror stories we had heard, was this all there was to it?

We were unnerved. I suppose we had good reason. The move was very important to us and we were playing with every penny we had. It was a big deal. At the same time we didn't want the worry to take over, and grow, and grind us to a halt. It was supposed to be an adventure, not a torture.

"I've got an idea,"I said. 'If the problem is that it seems too easy, why don't we make it harder?" A hair-shirt philosophy that has haunted me all my life; suffer a while before the pleasure.

"What do you have in mind?" Sandy asked.

"When you go back to England, I'll stay here. I'll take 'Blue', and comb the south coast from Provence down to the Spanish border. If we find something better, so be it. I don't think we will, but we'll know we had a good look. We'll have done some 'hard miles'."

"We're taking a chance. While you're doing that, someone else could buy the pink house."

"It's possible. Don't forget it's been for sale for four years. What's meant to happen is meant to happen, but I don't think we'll be gazumped."

Sandy stayed silent for a while, and then, "OK. It might be the answer. We'll look at the guide-books and choose a route. Leave out the areas we know we can't afford. Take a month, and keep a diary. Let's see."

EN GARD

It wasn't cold feet. We'd had the love at first sight and the gut feelings. Now we had the pre-wedding nerves. Before the commitment, one last fling, which should confirm that there was nothing better out there and that we had made the right choice.

We went our separate ways. Confident that our tastes were the same, I was to be a fine sieve, sifting out the boring, the dull and the downright ugly. I wouldn't see Sandy again for a month. By the time we met again I would have travelled 8,000 kilometres. Using a variation of her infamous grid system, I went from Provence to the Pyrenees-Orientales, never more than two hours drive from the coast. Lost in cork orchards, fattened on goose, propositioned by smugglers, massacred by mosquitoes, I did the 'hard miles'. I saw lovely houses in dying villages. I saw beautiful villages in spoilt countryside. Glorious landscapes were too isolated, pretty towns full of coaches and candyfloss. Even in France, where bargains were still to be had, perfect packages were too much money for us.

Sometimes I hugged the coast for days, abandoning the odious grid. There were no houses to research, no villages at all in the Petite Camargue. It was wild and lonely marshland and saltwater lagoons, best explored on horseback. A safe place for migrating birds to flock, and a permanent home for herons and flamingoes It was a breath of fresh air. Unless I wanted a salt pan or a rice farm, there was nowhere to buy. La Grande Motte was the opposite extreme. A resort with futuristic architecture, all pyramids and ziggurats and potted palms; hundreds of apartments for sale. Towards Spain, Collioure and Banyuls-sur-Mer were places that deserved more time than I could give them. The warm sea and grilled sardines and an evening promenade would be best shared anyway.

When the month was nearly up, Sandy threw in a few wild cards that had caught her eye; choosing villages, as she chose Grand National winners, because she liked their names. Prats-de-Mollo, St Guilhem-le-Desert and St Hippolyte-du-Fort, and a town called Joyeuse – a town called 'Cheerful', that made me thoroughly miserable.

I had kept a simple diary of the trip. Often one word was

enough for total recall – "360°", "Candyfloss", "cherries", "Brummies". When Sandy came back we sorted through the list, and I put flesh on the bones of names and places. There had been nothing and nowhere better than the pink house in the Gard. So, 8,000 kilometres and a month later, the last fling flung, we went back to Madame de la Fuente and asked, if the house was still unsold, to see it for the third time.

"Bien sur," she said "Friday afternoon is good for me – we'll have lunch first. I will ask the owner to join us at the house, with that key."

THE THIRD VISIT & THE BID

WE HAD MADE up our minds. This third visit to the house was to be for the pleasure of it, and to sustain us for a couple of months back in England, including Christmas.

Lunch with Madame de la Fuente was a *plat du jour*, duck breasts with a glass of wine. For the first time, the main topic of conversation wasn't the house. We filled in some details of our lives up to then, and why we were making the move from England. Our disaffection with a society based on political correctness and driven by greed. We remember it being our first serious French conversation, just about at the limit of our vocabulary. In return we learned that she was a grandmother and a bad golfer.

Mme de la F. had arranged to meet the owner at the house, with the elusive key. We disliked him on sight, another one of those gut feelings. This was made worse when he proceeded to tell us what we should do to the house. Put in a mezzanine floor here (get lost, I thought, that's a splendid high ceiling), knock down the top third of the house and put in a sun terrace, take out the apex on this roof and make it sloping, with a Velux window (bugger off; that's vandalism). Relationships deteriorated further when he admitted he hadn't brought the key.

"Sandy has just flown 1,000 miles to see THE WHOLE PROPERTY, Madame, including the garage!!!" I was clearly furious.

In a machine-gun burst of French between Mme de la F. and the owner, I gathered she was too. When I'm angry I can create an evil atmosphere, like releasing a foul-smelling gas. The owner had smelt it.

"I'll throw in that piece of land," he said, indicating a patch of grass and weeds about the size of a tennis court opposite the gates. He glanced at his watch.

"*Merde!* I must go. I'm late for an appointment," he said and left, without the polite formalities, to escape the gas and to avoid compromising his precious sale any further.

"I'm so sorry. He is a very..." Mme de la F. paused to choose her words carefully, '...particular sort of man."

Later we were to find out how particular.

"At least he has given you the parcel of land. You could make a little garden there; some melons perhaps..." She was trying to save the day.

Aside to Sandy I said quietly, "He just made a blunder. I'll explain later," and I thought about playing poker for a living.

"If we can't see the garage, perhaps we can look around the house again?" I asked.

Mme de la F. led the way.

"We should keep this as the kitchen," said Sandy. "The fireplace is a great feature, or would be without the brown paint. The room is..."

She didn't finish the sentence, but stared at the wall transfixed. I followed her gaze. Against the pale stone, at about shoulder height, was a black scorpion about two inches long with its tail curved over its back. As a child in the Middle East I had a collection of live scorpions. One escaped and found its way into my parents' marble bathtub; after which I collected butterflies. As an adult my attitude was different; I looked for something to kill it with.

"A scorpion!" Sandy said in disbelief.

"Where?" said Madame de la Fuente. I was still looking for a weapon when Mme de la F. leaned to her left from the waist, extended her arms for balance, and shot out her right leg at shoulder height, to crush the scorpion with her 3,000FF loafers. Pure Kung-fu. She said dismissively,

"They're in all stone houses. They're harmless, like a bee-sting. You learn to live with them."

We couldn't get into the garage, but I wanted to get a different view of the house by standing on its roof. As I climbed out onto it I heard a child's voice behind me, from the terrace next door.

'What are you doing here?" she demanded, hands on hips.

"Nothing mademoiselle," I said as I turned, surprised at her hostility. "I'm looking at this house, that's all."

THE THIRD VISIT & THE BID

"Don't you dare come up here!" she shouted, pointing to some steps which joined the flat roof to their terrace.

"I am interested in this house, not yours, mademoiselle," I said, annoyed by the little tyke.

She called for reinforcements. A young man stripped to the waist came onto the terrace from the house. He had not shaved for a week, and he flexed his muscles and scowled at me. I scowled back. He took a good long look and went back indoors without saying a word. Mademoiselle flounced off after him. I climbed back into our house and thought 'nice neighbours'.

We'd been a bit unlucky with neighbours over the years. Drunks, nymphomaniacs, moaners and bores – it didn't look as if things were going to change.

Visit over, we told Madame de la Fuente that we'd be making an offer over Christmas, wished her a merry one and went our separate ways. I was driving back to England that week. Sandy was flying back to work later that night and we set off towards the airport. On the way she asked what I had meant about the owner making a blunder.

"It's like a game of poker," I said, "and it's as if he's given us a sixth card to better his hand of five cards. We could put in a bid, without specifying if we include or exclude the land."

As we got close to the airport I had to get something off my chest.

"We really are going to come and live in France. You know we're going to have to tell the 'aged parents'? It won't be easy. I'm dreading it."

"Me too." said Sandy.

Back in England we had some sums to do, including guestimations about costs of materials and living expenses. Exchange rates were monitored like blood pressure in intensive care. Things were about to get complicated. We were to make an offer in one currency and have it accepted in another. The French franc was giving way to the Euro.

In our fax to Mme de la F., we said how much we loved the house. We had thought long and hard, and, in light of the magnitude of work, we could not pay the asking price. Instead we wished to formally offer £43,000. Wishing her season's greetings, we looked forward to hearing from her soon.

From the point at which we had first seen the house, there had been a currency swing in our favour. We had not specified whether or not the land was included in the offer. It seemed a bold bid. Now there was nothing for us to do but wait. And, of course, break the news to our mothers about what we'd done and what we were planning to do.

Dividing ourselves between families as fairly as possible over Christmas and New Year, it happened to be me who broke the news first.

"Duchess," I said tensely, "Sandy and I are buying a house in France. We're going to live there."

"All right, love. Any chance of a lift to bingo – I think it's come on to rain."

It was as simple as that. Perhaps because I'd left home to go to university, and had lived hundreds of miles away ever since, she was used to not having me around. London, Brighton or France, I still wasn't coming to tea on Sundays.

Sandy went through the same mill.

"Oh, thank goodness for that!" said Pooh, a mother of very big brain. "I thought you'd never do anything interesting again."

Bless them for making it easy.

We caught letters as they came through the door each morning and my brother checked our e-mail every evening. My birthday on December 22nd came and went. Sandy said a house in the south of France would have been a lovely birthday present. Demons came to visit; hissing in my ear that there were other buyers, and that I'd been greedy and foolish and a lousy poker player. We had a blistering chicken vindaloo to burn away the gloom.

Out and about the next day, we found a tiny internet café over a 24/7 Indian supermarket, sharing its premises with a seamstress whose toddler ran amok in a dirty nappy. I left Sandy to check e-mail and stayed with 'Blue'.

She is a woman who never runs if she can walk, and never walks if she can dawdle. Seeing Sandy in the rear-view mirror, in

THE THIRD VISIT & THE BID

full flight, I knew we had an answer. She collapsed against the side of the van and held out a piece of paper,

"He's said yes!" she blurted.

"The owner accepts your offer, but at this price he withdraws the offer of the land in the sale."

The relief was immediate. The pleasure too, but deep and quiet rather than fireworks and Irish jig. We were happy, and drained to danger point at the same time.

We e-mailed Mme de le F. and said simply "Wonderful news!"

"I didn't get the house for my birthday, but we've both got it for Christmas," I said.

"Let's collect the turkey and buy a bottle of bloody champagne."

After the holiday we had another message from Madame de la Fuente. The owner was willing to sell us the land separately if we wanted it. And she couched the offer in terms that left us in no doubt that he was being unreasonable,

"He will not consider offering the tiny piece of land for less than 3000 Euros."

We thought we had already squeezed the owner's pips on the house. We were feeling magnanimous.

"Let's just pay him what he wants for the land and be done with it," said Sandy.

We thanked Mme de la F. for her advice, but thought it was worth it to have all that space opposite the gates. For melons, as she had suggested, or fruit trees, or sunflowers. It was the making of the house, *'la cerise sur le gateau'*, and hoped that meant the same in French.

"One more thing," I said to Sandy as she typed, "we should ask her what on earth happens next?"

THE CONTRACT TO BUY

IN THE FIRST week of January, we heard that the owner would sell us the house and the land at the agreed prices. The next step was the *'Compromis de Vente'*; the equivalent of the English exchange of contracts. This would commit us to buying and the owner to selling, with deposits and hefty penalties for withdrawal.

Everyone curbed their impatience, juggled work schedules and travel arrangements, and settled on January 19th as the date for the *'compromis'* to be signed.

The meeting was arranged for the afternoon. This would give her a chance to introduce us to the mayor, check that the village had a sewer system for us to plumb into, collect a photocopy of the village plan with plot numbers, and to make sure the house was as we had last seen it. In the mushrooming architectural salvage business, stone fireplaces and staircases carried a premium on the black market.

I took the van back to France, and met Sandy from the airport on the 18th. The next morning went smoothly. All the lovely features were still in place, and so was all the rubbish. The mayor was not available, but his assistant welcomed us and answered all our questions, confirming that there were sewers throughout the village. Madame de la Fuente went off to lunch, and we sat in the Café de l'Industrie, watching the market packing up, too apprehensive to eat.

We arrived in her office at five to two, Mme de la F. at five past, the owner at twenty past, and the notaire didn't arrive at all. He had more pressing business. For my part I couldn't imagine anything more pressing than our *'Compromis de Vente'*.

'No matter," said Mme de la F, clearly fuming. 'I shall do it myself." She led the way to her back office, and we followed, armed with Collins Roberts French dictionary, about the size of a

THE CONTRACT TO BUY

small family saloon. 'The dictionary the world has trusted for over twenty years' it boasted on the cover; high recommendation for the afternoon of January 19th, 2002.

Madame opened a pre-printed book of numbered *'Compromis'*. Sandy's heart sank. Mme de la F. had started to fill in number 13, with the date and names and addresses. She made a small mistake, but as the document must be completed without errors and corrections, she was obliged to start again. We became number 14.

The vendor, Mr Vertigo as we called him in a corruption of his family name, tried two tricky manoeuvres. Firstly, under the property description, he wanted to call our house a ruin. Neurotically, this would reduce any liability that might come his way after the sale.

"No, monsieur. The house is not a ruin. I did not sell these people a ruin. It is a house with everything to do – *'tout a faire'* – but it is not a ruin. Not at all."

I felt as if we had Boadicea at the head of our army. Vertigo's mobile phone rang and he disregarded all of us, and spoke for a long time. Mme de le F. watched him with distaste. We really didn't like this man.

When it came to price details, Vertigo tried to pull his second trick.

"Put down that the price of the house is less, and the price of the land is more. It makes no difference, the total remains the same," he said slyly. Boadicea climbed into her chariot.

"Monsieur," she said, and from the expression on her face, I thought Vertigo should watch out, "Monsieur, I have written to these people and agreed with them a price for the house. And I have also agreed a price for the land. I have written to you and you know the prices. I will not change them now."

"What difference does it make? The total is the same," he persisted, not noticing the need to keep his head down.

"I will terminate this meeting if you continue, Monsieur," Madame removed her spectacles.

What she knew, of course, was his intention to lessen his tax liability on the separate sales. She was having none of it, the warrior queen.

"It is your responsibility, as the vendor, to supply the termite certificate," she went on.

"Termites!" Sandy and I cried simultaneously.

"The government requires that a house of this age and construction has a certificate from a specialist, who has checked for infestation. Termites are not a problem in this area, but the government insists. It is just a formality," Mme de le F. explained.

Between more interruptions from his mobile phone, we completed the process without any more attempts to cook the books. Each page was initialled by all of us, and with final signatures we were locked into the deal. Vertigo shot out of the door, without shaking our hands. Madame de le Fuente kissed us on both cheeks. It was done and she was pleased for us.

"We really need to thank you for what you did today," I said

"Non, Monsieur Scott, you don't need to thank me. It is a pleasure. You are both 'sympa.'"

I took it that Vertigo was not.

Money would fly about in the meantime, but we would not meet again until the *'Acte de Vente'* on April 19th. Much would happen before then.

BETWEEN EXCHANGE & COMPLETION
(Between the Devil and the deep blue sea)

SANDY FLEW BACK to England and I was to follow in 'Blue', stopping off in Normandy to spend some time on the boat. January in Fécamp would be very different from the Gard, all herrings and howling gales, gathering storms over slate fish-scale roofs. Ragged elms full of rooks' nests marched across muddy fields, like dishevelled conscripts with their shirts hanging out. On a sunny day, the sky was a thin meatless broth, streaked with greasy clouds. All kinds of dirty white; nothing on the tonal scale above a deep dove-grey. No-one had time to talk, hurrying to get home out of the wind and rain. Shops closed early, cafés not much later. It was lonely and melancholy, and not like 'home'.

On the trip north I had taken my time. We seemed to have been rushing around for months, and it was a pleasant change not to be tied to meetings and appointments. Outside Lyon I chose a small *aire*, to eat and sleep and to use the showers in the morning. 'Blue' was dwarfed among the long-distance lorries and trucks from all over Europe.

In the morning, I knelt to pee in the chemical loo. Still innocent with sleep, it took me a moment to realise that I was peeing in public; the van's sliding door was open.

"I've never left that unlocked before. I must have been more tired than I thought," I said out loud.

A hot shower followed by a hot breakfast and then back on the road, I thought, and looked around for my clothes. No jeans. No jacket. I hadn't left the door open. The van had been broken into while I slept. They had grabbed the two pieces of clothing in which most men carry around their lives – wallets, loose money, credit cards, driving licence, passport – and left me with my boots and T-shirt. Luckily 'Blue' was a wardrobe too, and I found other clothes and went to phone the gendarmes. I was angry, but the main feeling was one of disbelief. It's true I do sleep deeply, but it seemed incredible that I hadn't been woken; the sliding door makes a noise like thunder. On my way to the phone, I noticed trailers with half-open doors – I wasn't the only victim. I woke the truck drivers with the bad news. They cussed in Spanish or Serbo-Croat, angry at the delay and the police paperwork that was going to ruin their day.

When they eventually arrived, the gendarmes dealt with me quickly. A list of the stolen goods was taken – my battered old flying-jacket, some sweaty Levis, about 100 Euros and a plastic box full of change for the motorway tolls. Luckily my bank card had fallen on the floor, as it often did when I threw my jeans over the front seat, and my passport was with the ferry ticket, in an overhead locker. The two young policemen looked bored, when I said, over and over, that I couldn't believe I had slept through it.

"They are expert, Monsieur. It is an industry around here," one of them said. They handed me all the bits of paper my insurers would need, and moved on to the truckers. Matter closed.

I spent a week in Normandy, and drank a lot of cider to keep cheerful. Satisfied that I had fine-tuned the boat's moorings as well as I could, I pumped her dry and scrubbed the decks. The van was stocked with wine and some whisky and I caught the ferry to England. It wasn't long before I was reminded why we had left.

Sandy was working in London and living with her mother during the week. For the next couple of months we would see each other only at weekends. I would stay in the van in Brighton, using friends' bathrooms or the swimming-pool showers, and do my research into roofing and plumbing in the local library. Being by the sea was better than being in London.. Parked for free on the seafront, rocked to sleep at night by the wind and eating a lot of pizzas, I was quite happy. It was a compromise for us, but only until April.

The first weekend we had together we went for a long walk on the beach, and then made our way back into town along the high street.

"Want to buy tickets for the concert tonight?" asked a local 'crusty', one of the hundreds of beggars who have decided that there's a good living to be made in a day-tripper town like Brighton. He was stumbling about with a bottle of White Lightning, grinning at us with broken brown teeth.

"No thanks, mate," I said, without stopping. "We won't be here." We were planning to drive out to a country pub for dinner.

"No you won't, 'cause I'm gonna kick your fuckin' arses right out of this town, you bastards!" he shouted after us, staggering back to his friends in a doorway.

I turned to look at him, remembering all the times I'd been asked for money in the streets here. Often every hundred yards, until my pockets were empty or I felt resentful enough to refuse. A refusal sometimes provoked a sarcastic crack, sometimes they threw a pebble or an empty can of lager. This had been part of everyday life, until I was desensitised enough not to think twice about it. But I'd been in France for a while, and had been re-sensitised. Roll on April.

A fortnight later, Sandy had days off in the middle of the week. I wanted a swim and a shower, and mid-week was usually a good time. We arrived at the pool early; it was 'women only' before 10.30am. The only parking spot big enough for the van was against some railings around a children's' playground. It was playtime and the kids were wrapped up warm against the February winds. They were delightful and funny; hats falling over their eyes, tripping over long scarves and playing tag. We watched them and laughed. Sandy pointed out the lonely little girl who stood apart and said sadly that there was always one in any group. I started to write out a list of things we needed for the van and handed it to Sandy to add to. There was a knock on the passenger-door window and a matronly woman stood there motioning us to wind the window down.

"One of my teachers has been to see me. We are very concerned about your behaviour around these children. You have been watching them for a long time, and talking about them and writing things down about them. What is your interest? What are you doing here?" she asked, her eyes everywhere inside the van. It was like being punched. We knew exactly what she was implying.

"We're waiting to go for a swim, not that it's any of your busi-

EN GARD

ness," Sandy replied in a trembling voice.

"Then why don't you go for your swim?" the woman asked coldly.

"No men allowed before 10.30," I said angrily. 'No men allowed to sit in camper vans. No men allowed to look at children. No men allowed, anywhere. No men allowed."

"I was hoping for your understanding in this," the woman said. "We have to be very careful in the current climate."

She didn't say it, but she meant that the world was full of monsters; us for example.

I got up to get my towel and bag.

"You don't have my understanding. You have my sodding rage!" I said and slammed out of the van towards the pool. The woman took a few steps back, away from this monster.

"Look," said Sandy showing her our shopping-list, "This is what we were writing. See – matches, washing-up liquid, kitchen roll. What ugly minds you all have. You make me feel sick. Please go away..." and she started to cry quietly.

Sandy had taken an awful blow. As a man in England I knew it was dangerous to touch and talk to children, even if they needed help; for my own protection I had withdrawn from any contact over the last few years. It was overwhelmingly sad to have had a child snatched away by its mother, after I'd found it lost and crying in a supermarket. No word of thanks, just a look of total loathing. I stopped trying after that. But this was Sandy's first brush with the paranoia and she took it badly.

We had been sitting in a van, all the doors and windows closed, number plate clearly visible. We were in a busy public place, in broad daylight. We had not tried to make any contact with any of the children. Yet somehow we were guilty of something. I wanted to remind those teachers with their concerns about us, that most harm is done to kids by people they know – their family, their neighbours and even their teachers. Roll on April.

We only stayed in Brighton after that because Sandy was preparing an exhibition of jewellery for the Brighton Festival. There were some lovely evenings with her friend Jackie, who had taught her silver-smithing, and with Jackie's husband Rob. They redeemed the town for us. While the girls worked long hours in Jackie's studio, I enjoyed Rob's dry Northern humour as we cooked an evening meal. We bartered; his high-octane home brew bitter for our bottles of Côtes du Rhône.

On Easter weekend the girls decided to have Sunday off, and Sandy and I went for a drive in the van. Late afternoon we were looking for a place to park up for the night, and a good pub.

"I must call my mother tonight," said Sandy.

"Do it now," I told her, and I don't know why.

"She's having lunch at Keith's today. I'll do it later."

"No, call Keith's. Do it now."

When the phone was answered the other end, it was her nephew.

"Grandma's just leaving in an ambulance. I think it's a stroke. Mum and Dad are going with her. Thank God you phoned. Are you coming?"

We hammered 'Blue' up the motorway, thankful that we hadn't been drinking all day. What made me insist on the phone-call I'll never know.

Sandy's mother had suffered a major stroke. She had not regained consciousness and responded only by returning a squeezed hand. The doctor in intensive care was straightforward and honest. The next day or two were crucial. If she survived, she would probably be permanently disabled. She would have a brain-scan, to see which areas were damaged. But for now she would go to the special stroke unit, and we should prepare ourselves for the worst. Sandy had already decided to stay with her, and one phone call to her employers gave her all the time she needed. A bed was made up for her alongside her mother's, and I got special permission to sleep in the van, in the car park.

It was not to be over quickly. Keith and Lesley spent all their spare time at the hospital. Their kitchen and bathroom were at our disposal. We all got very close very quickly. Sandy was preoccupied with her mother's quality of life, if she survived. A thousand times she'd heard her say she'd rather be dead than a vegetable, and she knew her mother had been stockpiling paracetamol for years, just in case. I thought Sandy was magnificent. She kept her vigil, day and night, and said everything she wanted to say. I had less courage and less resilience. Keith too found it an agony. The two of us volunteered to repaint the nurses' rest room in a revolting livid violet. It distracted us enough to laugh for a couple of hours.

We had some decisions to make about the trip to France for the *'Acte de Vente'*, now only ten days away. It was agreed between all of us that we should still go, knowing that Pooh would have said, 'For goodness sake, get on with it."

Money was transferred to the notaire's account via a Guernsey bank, on schedule. I booked a ferry and Sandy booked her flights. The vigil went on.

The hospital had an internet café and I spent some time there each day. An e-mail arrived from Madame de la Fuente, telling us to contact our bank urgently, adding *'pas de inquietude'*. What was going on? The bank insisted there were no problems and so we were no wiser. We rang Mme de la F. and she asked if we knew what had happened.

"Madame, the bank says everything is fine."

"Fine? Except that they have paid for your house twice!"

The bank had acted on both the faxed instructions and the hard-copy which followed, and sent £46,000 in euros each time – and charged us twice for the privilege. Every time I have been £5 overdrawn, I have paid heavily. The bank never apologised. We were reimbursed in full of course, but it went no further than that. Nice work if you can get away with it.

On the eve of my departure, Pooh gave up her fight for life. Sandy and Keith were both there. I arrived minutes later. Empty of wise words, we cried and comforted ourselves with the knowledge that hers had been a long, full and happy life, surrounded by love.

"We can postpone the *'Acte de Vente,'*" I said.

"For goodness sake, let's just get on with it."

The genes live on...

We did have to arrange a postponed funeral to accommodate our trip. That done I headed off for France. Two days later I would be meeting Sandy at the airport, 1,300 kilometres further south.

THE ACTE DE VENTE

A VIRTUE OF using kilometres over long distances is that you seem to be getting somewhere faster. I was flat out in 'Blue' south from Calais. Meatloaf blasted me with 'Bat out of Hell' and strong black espresso kept me going. Around Lyon I was dangerously tired; the last two weeks had taken their toll. I'd been robbed on the outskirts of the city last time, but sure that lightning couldn't strike twice, I pulled into an *aire* for the night.

It was punishingly cold. The van was packed with bits and pieces for the house in France and the chemical loo was buried under some of them. I went for a pee behind the van barefoot, and for half an hour my feet ached. I got under the duvet fully-clothed and took a long time dozing off. I pulled my thermal jacket on top of the duvet for extra warmth and eventually slept.

I woke up with a hangover. And cold. My jacket had gone. It had happened again and this time it was more serious. My passport had been in the jacket pocket. I was due to fly back for Pooh's funeral in a week, and that week included a day with a notaire, and of course a Saturday and Sunday. Three hundred kilometres still to go to meet Sandy tonight, and now I'd have to wait for the gendarmes and go through their paperwork. I rang them and then I rang Sandy.

"I'll call the British Embassy in Paris and find out what we can do. Maybe they can give us a temporary passport. Don't worry. Have you got enough money? For diesel and food?"

"It was so cold I kept all my clothes on, and my money was in my jeans. I've got plenty to get me to Nîmes. Just don't know how long the police will take. If I'm not there when you land, wait – I'm on my way!"

Much later I learnt that these specialists, who prey on campers and caravans, leak a gas into the vehicles through sink outlets. It knocks out cold the occupants, and their pets. Hence my hangover.

Past Lyon and some heat started to come back into the sun. Red tiles and hill-top villages began to appear. This was more like it. I stopped for tuna in Provençal sauce and looked forward to a pastis. The bottle I had taken to England had tasted horrible, out of its natural habitat. I collected Sandy the Indomitable on time and we set off for Bagnols and a good night's sleep before another stressful day tomorrow. She had spoken to the Embassy, and if we had the necessary documents, the consulate in Marseille could give us a temporary travel document.

"What documents do they want?" I asked.

"Your birth certificate, your parents' birth certificates, and their wedding certificate."

"Well, God knows where they are? In a suitcase in storage in Brighton, I suppose. That's that."

"Oh no, they're not. They were in my room at my mother's. I was bringing them anyway – who knows what we're going to be asked for tomorrow, for identification, besides passports. Your parents' stuff was with your birth certificate. I just brought it all."

"Unbelievable. As long as things go smoothly, we can get down to Marseille after the weekend."

Out of the mouths of babes………

At the morning visit to the house, again to check that it hadn't been stripped out, we discovered that the owner had not been near the place since January. The broken chairs, yellowed newspapers, sacks of mushroomy clothing, rat skeletons, sacks of seeds and piles of ironmongery were just as we left them. He hadn't bothered to clear it out.

"That's good," said Sandy. 'I'm going to enjoy sorting through it all; and maybe he's leaving us those old stoves after all." She had her eye on them, but they weren't fixtures and fittings.

Madame de la Fuente tried her best to allay our apprehension about the legal process. Today was the culmination of so much and the start of so much more. We were otherworldly. Not with it at all. I'd better sharpen up. In the hushed offices of the notaire, whose half-moon glasses added gravitas to the whole thing, we left it to the experts to do their stuff. Mme de la F. took time to

THE ACTE DE VENTE

explain things if we asked. Just before the final page and the signatures, Vertigo's avocat intervened.

"My client," he announced, "requires time to empty the house. It is clear from the 'compromis' that the house is sold without goods and chattels."

Boadicea was back in armour. She announced that the proceedings would have to stop. We had visited the house that morning, and we were buying 'as was'. She made ready to leave. The avocat and the notaire had a heated discussion. Vertigo joined in; Mme de le F. too. Another date was suggested, and we refused it. He'd had three months and we thought that was enough. We had a funeral to go to, and work to return to. We weren't going to be bullied and we didn't like him. He was screwing up what should have been a great day in our lives, and it was unforgivable.

The notaire came up with a compromise. It was Friday today; Vertigo could have the weekend to clear the house. The *'Acte'* could go ahead with that codicil. If we agreed, then, on Monday, the house 'as was' would be ours.

"Only do this if you are completely happy," counselled Boadicea.

We agreed.

"I'm going to be at the house every minute of the weekend, and I'm going to watch him like a hawk," said Sandy, staring Vertigo down.

The house was ours, but we didn't have the keys. If we weren't already cried out, we would have wept. Madame de le Fuente did not make the mistake of underplaying the meeting and its effect on us.

"*Bon,*" she said. 'He has the weekend."

"I will be in your office on Monday. And then we shall have our home," I said and tried to keep my voice steady. It was as much a threat, as information. I hoped she would pass it on to Vertigo.

There was one more thing to do. We were obliged, as the new owners though not the new residents, to insure the house. Third party insurance, in case a tile fell on a neighbour's head. In the insurance office a notice board displayed local houses for sale through local agents.

"Look," said Mme de la F., pointing out a property smaller than ours, not so pretty, with no land, at twice the price.

"Yours is a beautiful house," she said. "*Bon courage; bon chance.*"

We drove to the village. Like prisoners on the outside wanting to get in, we parked on our little bit of France opposite the house, and looked at it through the locked gates. There was a melba of a sunset, and we sat on a village bench with a glass of wine. We were cheering up nicely when a young man came by.

"My mother asks if you would like to join her for a drink?" he asked, introducing himself as Djimmy, from the house next door. (The "D" before the "j" is a particular gypsy thing – like "Django Reinhardt".)

Fifteen years in Brighton and no neighbour ever invited us for a drink; fifteen minutes in the village and we had an invitation. This was, we agreed, exactly as we'd dreamt village life in France would be.

Djimmy held his arms and shoulders like a gun-slinger, and walked on the outside edge of his feet. He was handsome, with a winning smile. We followed him up steps to a terrace, past cages full of quails and canaries, and into the glaring light of a kitchen. He introduced us to Lola, his mother, a smouldering gypsy brunette with rock-babe make-up and a leather skirt. Its hem skimmed her bum, and she was smothered in gold jewellery.

"Please..." she pulled out two chairs. "Pastis?"

She poured without waiting for a reply, and called out in a husky foghorn, that we came to know so well, "Djojo! Carla!"

"My youngest son and daughter." She introduced them as they arrived, mouths covered in chocolate milk, eyes like saucers.

"I have already met mademoiselle," I said, and the little tyke blushed.

"So, are you on holiday?" Lola asked.

"No, Madame. We are your new neighbours. We have bought the house next door," I replied.

She let out a wail.

"Nooooooo! It's not possible!" We waited.

"How many times have I seen you at the house? I thought I should say something. 'I must go and speak with them', I said. I never did, and now it's too late!"

She was a gypsy in full flood, hands flying, hair tossing, eyes rolling. Another wail.

"Aaaaaaahhh! Tell me it's not possible? Tell me you can get your money back? There is still time – tell me!"

"Non, madame. Everything is signed. Today."

"*Ohhhhh non non non non non!*"

"Madame," said Sandy, a bit rattled, "what are you talking about? Why should we stop everything?"

"Because..." Lola panted slightly. Her hands came onto the table and formed claws.

"...Because..." she seemed to drag her body across the table with her talons, and her voice was a hiss,

"... Because you are dealing with the Devil." She clutched her left breast and her eyes were on fire.

"Oh, great!" said Sandy, falling back in her chair. I'm not sure where my own calm came from. Bone-marrow tiredness I expect.

"I don't know what you mean, Madame, but perhaps we can talk about it tomorrow? We are very tired. It has been a long day for us. Thank you for the pastis. We'll see you in the morning ... please excuse us now," I said, and we went back to the van.

"What on earth can she be talking about?" asked Sandy.

"I don't know. I really don't."

We went to bed and tried to comfort one another enough to sleep.

"Scotty, stop the roller-coaster for an hour or two," Sandy whispered.

I wished I knew how. I closed my eyes, but the Devil was everywhere in my head.

Saturday came and went; no Vertigo to collect his precious tat, no more revelations from the neighbours.

Sunday a truck turned up with two workmen, and Vertigo appeared soon after with his son. They emptied the attics of an old wooden high-chair, some glass flagons, and large picture frames. Anything they didn't want they piled in a heap among the brambles. When the pile was big enough Vertigo ordered his men to set fire to it.

EN GARD

"There will be no fire in our courtyard. Remove the rubbish or leave it where it is. No fire! Do you understand?" Sandy shouted at them; it was the moment when ownership of the house really changed hands. Much more significant than any *'Acte de Vente'*.

"I'll be back for the stoves on Monday," Vertigo said as he climbed into his car.

"Oh no, you bloody won't," said Sandy.

GIVE ME BACK MY GRANDMOTHER'S WARDROBE

ON MONDAY we would have to leave the house unattended when we went to collect the keys. To the padlock and bicycle chain Vertigo had on the gates, to keep us out, we added a padlock and chain to keep him out. It felt bad doing it. We had never imagined our house with locks and chains. Keeping people out was the exact opposite of what we wanted. Open house was what we had in mind, not closed doors. Vertigo was tainting everything.

We arrived late for our two o'clock appointment, and Madame de la Fuente was there before us. We were getting the hang of time in the Gard.

"The keys!" said Mme de la F, smiling broadly.

"*Enfin!*" I said, "We see inside the garage."

"*Non.* Not quite. There is a small problem."

Sandy groaned.

"And the small problem is?"

"The problem is that there are stolen goods in the garage. Monsieur Vertigo is absolutely sure about this and has informed the *gendarmerie*. Of course he no longer owns the house and so it is a bit complicated. The *gendarmes* have agreed to wait until this evening, at five o'clock. They will meet you at the house and you will give them access to the garage. They ask that you leave the doors locked until then. Once again Monsieur Vertigo has put me in a difficult position. Please accept my apologies." Madame de la Fuente looked embarrassed as she gave me the keys.

"I don't believe this." said Sandy. 'When Lola says we're dealing with the Devil, she must mean Vertigo."

Under-reacting as usual, we simply took the keys, grateful to have them in our hands at last. We said our goodbyes to Madame de la Fuente, not expecting to see her again for a while. Whatever Vertigo was playing at, it wasn't her fault. She had been nothing but kind, helpful and protective to us – it was unfortunate that her client was the Devil, but we had no reason to be angry with her. We wanted no ill-feeling between us, and asked her to drop in whenever she was passing the house.

"Stop. Stop. Stop..." I said a little way down the road. "I need a coffee and time to think. This is madness."

Sitting in the Café de l'Industrie we couldn't agree on what to do for the best.

"If there are stolen goods in the garage," Sandy said, "Vertigo put them there – he's the only one with a key."

"And why has he waited until today to tell the police?" I asked. "He was at the house with the key for hours yesterday, so why didn't he call the *gendarmes* then?"

"He's giving us the problem."

"Well, we can give it back to him. We take the keys back to the office. Whatever has been going on at the house before we bought it, it's nothing to do with us. I don't want us to arrive in the village with hordes of police. He called them, he can let them in," I said and put the keys on the table.

"Oh no, Scotty, let's just do what she said. I'm tired and I want my house. Give the keys to the police at five and let them do whatever they want. And then I'd like us to be left in peace."

"No, I don't want us arriving in the village like this. It's not how I imagined us starting out." I thought it would be an awful beginning. More than that, I did not want to do anything for Vertigo. In fact I wanted to stand up to him. Even to stand against him.

"Please, Sandy, take the keys back to Madame de la Fuente, and tell her we cannot, we will not, do this. And tell her why. Vertigo can do his own dirty work."

I sat and waited in the Cafè de L'Industrie. Sandy explained to Madame de la Fuente our feelings about bad beginnings and bad karma.

"Mr Vertigo is a horrible, devious man and we don't trust him. We don't know what this is all about, but it is none of our business. He has given us nothing but problems from the beginning. Now, when we should be free to enjoy our house, he's still making problems. Let him be there at five o'clock to deal with it."

GIVE ME BACK MY GRANDMOTHER'S WARDROBE!

Mme de la F. took the keys and understood completely. She did not think Vertigo would be able to come; she believed he had flown to Morocco that morning. With a big sigh she said she would be there herself at five o'clock to let the *gendarmes* in.

Early for the appointment, and not her usual relaxed self, she told us not to worry, it would not take long. She pursed her mouth into cod lips, shrugged deeply, and lit a cigarette.

"It is a lot of fuss about nothing."

I was not so sure. I thought I could be at war in a little while; on the front line too.

Gendarmes usually travel in pairs. For the 'fuss about nothing' two pairs arrived, trousers tucked into boots, wearing guns, wrap-around sunglasses and Gauloise moustaches. They spoke with Madame de la Fuente, telling each other what they knew. The shoulder-shrugging and head-shaking like the mating-dance of cranes. Madame de la Fuente handed over the keys to the *gendarme* with the largest and most splendid moustache, presumably the 'chief'.

The lock mechanism had rusted and would not budge. The stolen property must have been there a very long time. Before the *gendarmes* tried to kick the door down, I fetched some WD 40 from the van. I sprayed the lock, teased the mechanism and heard it click. Pushing wide the heavy door, I saw a beautifully vaulted room, stacked high with worthless junk. So much for Fagin's lair.

I didn't know what the stolen property was, but, in this rats' nest, it would not be easy to find. Three of the *gendarmes* set about looking, swearing under their breath and slapping the dust off their clean trousers There were musty bed bases under rotting mattresses, 1950s furniture heaped everywhere – all veneer and brass, plastic bags with clothing spilling out, one splendid wardrobe riddled with worm, cardboard boxes split by age, bits of workshop machinery, parts of ladders, a broken television set, kids' shoes, a three-legged sofa with rusty springs – and plenty of other chipped, cracked, smashed and rotting rubbish under all that. Over everything, including the gendarmes, like a fall of silky snow, there were several hundredweights of grey dust.

Not long after the *gendarmerie* had arrived, the whole village

EN GARD

knew there was a scene at the end of the lane, opposite the Temple. Old fellows in their slippers and old ladies in their spotless aprons, determined not to miss a thing, gathered at the top of the gentle incline thirty yards away, and strained to see and hear. The mayor turned into the village in his car but could not get round the police van. Instead, he got out and came into the courtyard to make himself known. He spoke first of all to the 'chief', and then came towards me.

"Monsieur Scott. Welcome to the village!" If there was sarcasm, it was wasted on me.

The neighbours' guard dog was going berserk. The whole family came onto their terrace to find out why, and to hush the din. They could not miss the commotion in the courtyard, the crowd of spectators and the police vehicle. Lola came down, all fired up. When she saw the open garage door and the three *gendarmes* inside, she demanded to know what was going on. She and the 'chief' seemed to know each other quite well.

"We've had information, Madame, that there is stolen property here. My men are searching for it now," the chief told her.

She barked, louder than her dog had ever barked, at the men inside the garage,

"Non!!! Don't you dare touch anything! Get away from there!" There was menace. The brown eyes blazed. Madame de la Fuente was all calm assurance.

"Madame," she said, "please control yourself. This is a matter for the police. They are looking for something and..."

"Don't you call me 'Madame' in that tone of voice. Who are you anyway? You work for Vertigo don't you? I've seen you here before. You work for that Devil! Don't speak to me! What do you want with my things?"

"Madame, let me explain," started Madame de la Fuente, still calm, but now biting her lip.

The men roundabout were silent, cowed even, and peripheral.

"Explain? Explain! Yes, yes, please explain why the police are going through my things. What are they looking for? This perhaps..." screamed Lola. She held up a pretty little frock. "This was my daughter's dress, my DISABLED daughter's dress, when she

GIVE ME BACK MY GRANDMOTHER'S WARDROBE!

was a baby. Or this perhaps..." she grabbed a photo album, falling apart at the seams and waved it in Madame de la Fuente's face.

"...there is nothing to 'look' for here. It is Vertigo making trouble again. He has stored our things and he won't give them back. Not just us, other people too. Those people there in the street – go and ask them." She was sobbing now and cradling in her arms some baby clothes, using a tiny sleeve to wipe away tears.

"That Devil," she wailed "he is the thief!"

"Madame, stop this," said de la Fuente and her face pulsed red. She reached out a hand to touch Lola's shoulder and stay the ranting.

"Don't you dare touch me," said Lola through gritted teeth.

''Oh, my God, there's going to be a fight!'' I thought, sure that fur was going to fly.

The 'chief', who was not getting his hands dirty in the search, directing operations leaning on the door-jamb, recovered his authority in the nick of time and stepped between the women.

"Enough! That is enough!" He meant it, too.

"Monsieur!" He called me to him. "You have bought this house?"

"*Oui*, monsieur," I didn't know what else to call a policeman in France. "Last Friday."

Mme de le F. explained the complications. The *gendarme* thought for a while. He was getting bored, and if it was a choice between a bit of overtime or a pastis...

"Then, as far as I can see, you have bought the house and everything in it. All these things are yours."

"Naaaaaaaaaaaaaaaaaaa!" wailed Lola. It was animal, loud and long.

From inside the garage, the dustiest gendarme called out,

"Chief! I have found the stolen property!" and he held up a disintegrating cardboard box, containing a dozen Fernandel video cassettes.

"All this is about a few videos?" I said, to anyone who might share my disbelief.

An old lady was knocking at the gate.

"*Oui?*" I said without much grace, thinking I had enough on my plate.

"Please, Monsieur, give me back my grandmother's wardrobe!" She was crying too.

"Of course you may have your grandmother's wardrobe, Madame. Please don't upset yourself. And thank you – you have given me an idea."

I called over the chief.

"I have bought the house and everything in it – isn't that true?"

He nodded, stroking his moustache.

"Well, I have no need of any of these things, and would like to give them away to anyone who wants them."

The *gendarme* saw the same way out of the mess, and a way out of the cat-fight.

"One more thing," I tried, "if I have bought everything, and in good faith, then the videos are no longer stolen goods, they are bought goods. Perhaps the matter is closed?"

The *gendarme* needed to leave his mark on the proceedings, and bring them to an end.

"In that case," he said to all and sundry, "everything in this garage has to be moved in twenty minutes. After that time, anything that remains belongs to the Englishman."

Without waiting for the twenty minute deadline, the *gendarmes* left. I left, too, to fetch a bottle of pastis from the van. It seemed the only sensible thing to do. Sandy had stayed in the van throughout, too upset to get involved. She came back to the house with me and the pastis. I explained the compromise.

"So, the whole stolen property thing was just Vertigo poisoning the day? Lola's right – he is the Devil."

Lola called her family to clear the garage of all their things. First I helped them carry out the old lady's splendid wardrobe, ruined by worm. When she saw the state of it, the old lady wept inconsolably, shaking the gates and looking heavenward she cried,

"*Grandmère*, I'm so sorry, please forgive me!" It was pretty distressing stuff. I called to everyone.

"Let's just stop for a while. Forget about the twenty minutes. It doesn't matter. Let's have a pastis together – except that I don't have enough glasses." Glasses appeared from everywhere, and

GIVE ME BACK MY GRANDMOTHER'S WARDROBE!

bottles of cold water to go with the pastis.

I invited Lola to one side.

"Lola," I said, "I am so sorry that this has happened. I want you to know that it had nothing to do with us."

"Of course it had nothing to do with you. It is the work of the Devil."

"I think you're right," I said.

With the pastis and the amount of furniture, the job of emptying the garage was left half done. People drifted away. Show over. In the street, against the garage wall, for collection in the morning, were propped the bed bases and their mattresses, and sacks of clothing. I hated it that little intimacies were on such public display. I found a child's pink shoe. There was a neat knot where the matching lace had been repaired. I put it in one of the sacks for collection. The courtyard was littered with empty pastis glasses, as it would be many times in the future.

"Scotty, we really do live here now," said Sandy.

That felt about right. There's just the trip to Marseille and the funeral, I thought and tried to unwind.

We made Marseille and back the next day. I was given a travel document, which would have to be surrendered to immigration on arrival. I would need a new passport for the return trip.

There were two days before we flew back to England, and we wanted to make a start on the house in some small way. To leave our mark on it.

I had promised the brambles they would be my first job. They stood up to our chests, had tendrils twenty feet long, main branches thicker than Cumberland sausages and roots that sucked moisture from Australia. They were vicious and all but stopped us getting to and from the main house.

"Slash and burn," said Sandy after thinking over the problem. "You slash and I'll burn."

She found an old galvanised dustbin in the house and emptied out the almond husks. We knocked through some holes and that was the incinerator. Ferry-terminal security had been slack, and I had brought with me in the van two rusty, trusty short-handled scythes that had belonged to Sandy's grandad. I set to work with them.

I slashed the brambles and the brambles slashed me. After four hours all that was left were countless stalks sticking out of the earth, perfect handholds for lifting the roots. What an optimist. Even the roots had thorns and, after another couple of hours, I was covered in bloody scratches, especially my hands. My face had caught a few whiplashes and was a mess too.

"What a sight you're going to look at the funeral," Sandy laughed.

"You don't look much better yourself!" The cuts were stinging from the salt in my sweat. April sun means hot sun here.

We bought *croissants* for the first time in the village *boulangerie*, took a paraffin stove from the van to make coffee, and in the middle of the afternoon, had our first 'breakfast' in our house.

In the garage we took down cobwebs big enough to trap gazelles. Sandy didn't want to think about what might have lived in them. We swept and dusted like *hausfraus*, and washed the floor with disinfectant. Towards evening, the room was fresh and clean. It was nine metres long and six metres wide – twice the size of the living room in Brighton.

"We can live quite happily in this," said Sandy.

We set about doing just that. Crockery and cutlery made their way over from the van. Lola had left a plastic table and chairs outside the gates – "just in case you need them". Sandy emptied spaghetti sauce into a pan, washed out the jar, filled it with water and set off down the lane to pick wild flowers for her 'vase'.

En Gard, en fin.

May 2002
Turning on the tap

Den,
We have water. Just the one outside tap, but it is available at the twist of a wrist. No more twelve mile trips to fill up jerry cans from a street pump. No more rationing. It must have been like this when cavemen discovered fire. No more flints and rubbing sticks, and cursing the rain for damp twigs. Hours saved and one thing less to worry about. There is a fountain here in the village, that pours into the old wash-house, but not recommended for drinking – not without adding pastis.

We also have a rat. As well as a bat, and a cat. Spent days trying to convince ourselves that it was a very big mouse. Deep down we always knew. It comes into the garage at night and runs along moonlit shelves, rustling about amongst the tools; wonder what it makes of the rat-tail file? It may have been driven indoors by the heavy rain. I suppose the garage looks dry and welcoming, even luxurious, if your nest has floated away down a drain. This is the heart of the country after all, we shouldn't be surprised. It's probably more 'Wind in the Willows' than Stephen King. Still, it is a rat and I don't know if I can live with it. Hope so; last thing I want to do is start killing off local wildlife.

The bat is tiny, a pipistrelle we think. It comes out just after the sun goes down, swooping and flitting; making short work of moths and other night-life. To think I used to watch television in the evenings.

The cat is feral and very pregnant. She's chosen 'the studio' for her confinement. We're feeding her, which might be a mistake. Far too wild to be a pet, our only contact is over a bowl of food, with lots of ungrateful hissing. I hiss back. The village feral tom, whom we assume is the father, is a handsome devil; film-star good looks. Part Siamese we guess, with a creamy Wilton carpet coat, Paul Newman's eyes and stripey socks. She is small and slender; her coat a mix of grey and ginger, which looks pink in some lights. We can't wait to see the kittens that come from that gene pool.

EN GARD

Scorpion season too. After days of dutifully knocking out my trainers each morning, with nothing to show for it but a couple of woodlice, this morning a black scorpion fell out. It adopted the usual body-builder pose – pincers akimbo, sting and tail arched – and then scuttled away as fast as six legs could carry it. They are completely non-aggressive. As a Scorpio astrologically, under the impression that I am a nasty piece of work, with a dark side and a sting in my tail, I don't see that in scorpions at all. They just want to be left alone.

Now we have water, I have planted a few things. Nothing like a lick of paint and some flowers for instant gratification. Bearing in mind where work will be starting – tramping feet and falling mortar and ladders – the flowers are in pots. Moveable feasts of nasturtiums and geraniums, and a couple of honeysuckle in the dappled corner. Huge temptation to go for bougainvillea and hibiscus, because we've come South. But this is a frost pocket that would cut them off at the knees.

What was good in Brighton is probably good here – although that did include passionflowers and lilies, which are hardly second best. Our mayor stopped by today to admire the pots by the gates and the new shutters. Pleased to see the eyesore at the end of the village in caring hands at last.

Scotty chats away to him; his French is good, after just a couple of months. I trail along behind, strangled by verbs and masculine and feminine nouns. Pronunciation is a baited trap. I once went market shopping in Rome and asked for 'a nice fresh tortoise' instead of a nice fresh lettuce; I couldn't sleep because gypsies, rather than mosquitoes, were flying round the room all night. Here we have seen a beautiful church in a hammock, and are thinking of buying a frying pan to keep us warm this winter. It keeps people entertained, and they politely put us straight. They are charmed but we are not ridiculed. I love words so much, it's like having my head cut off, not to be able to say exactly what I want; to be floundering, like a five year old. Not being fluent is torture.

There is a huge curiosity about us, and the old ladies' evening stroll makes a point of passing our gates. At first we nodded. Then we exchanged hellos. Each day the banter lasts longer. A young man stopped outside, he likes the colour of the gates; he nearly crashed his car when he saw them, no longer tangled by fig trees or streaked in rust.

I am back to work this weekend and will miss our first village party.

TURNING ON THE TAP

Scotty is going with the neighbours. Their third son has asked him to be his partner in the boules match. A small gesture that almost makes your heart burst. He is practising his 'long game' now, and the cries of 'Merde!' echo off the temple walls.

Look forward to pictures of the new kitten – called what? You can let your imagination take fire naming a cat – something herbal or spicy or astronomic or historic; certain that you'll never have to call it across a field or crowded park. You can't have too much of a mouthful with a dog. We miss not having one, but with the French version of the RSPCA on the doorstep, who knows what may happen...

All love from us both

xxxxxx

THE SISTERS-IN-LAWS' RABBIT STEW

WE COLLECT COLLECTIVE nouns. After a day with your head in a cement mixer, playing with language is hands-off, hands-clean exercise.

It helps us keep a toehold on English too, saturated as we are by French. Losing a grip on your mother tongue, before you have a firm grasp of another, is to feel like a verbal refugee.

A quire of angels; a horde of misers; a mass of priests – a game with words that won't translate. Proper collectives, a parliament of owls and a murder of crows and an unkindness of ravens, are unexplainable; losing everything in the translation.

I once won a scrabble game with 'nye', the collective noun for pheasants. It nearly got me lynched. Nobody likes a clever dick.

In the village, we have 'a bench of sisters-in-law', who collect every evening. This is their recipe for rabbit, with family variations. It is basically a hunter's stew. The herbs could be picked from underfoot, as you made your way home with a couple of rabbits in your pouch.

You will need: a rabbit cut into pieces, 4 oz stoned prunes, ½ pint each red wine and chicken stock, 3oz stoned black olives, 5 oz streaky bacon in inch long pieces, 2 tbsp. olive oil, 1 tbsp. flour, bouquet garni, salt and pepper.

For the marinade: ½ pint red wine, 2 tbsp. oil, 1 large onion & 1 large carrot, both chopped roughly, 12 peppercorns and a bayleaf.

A flameproof casserole dish and a large china dish for the marinade. A serving dish.

Mix the marinade and add the rabbit and prunes. Stir it well and leave somewhere cool overnight.

Use a slotted spoon to remove the rabbit, prunes and vegetables from their marinade and dry them with kitchen paper. Putting the oil in the casserole, first brown the rabbit and then the vegetables.

Remove the meat, sprinkle the flour over the vegetables and

THE SISTERS-IN-LAWS' RABBIT STEW

sauté for a minute or two.

Stir in the marinade, wine and stock and add the bouquet garni, garlic and seasoning.

Return the meat to the casserole and bring to the boil.

Cover and simmer for 30 minutes or so.

Dry fry the bacon and add, together with the prunes and olives, and continue cooking for another 15 minutes.

If the juices haven't thickened enough for your liking, remove the rabbit and vegetables to the serving dish and boil the liquid until it forms a sauce.

Madame Gouderch likes to flambé the rabbit in cognac. Madame Ekel stirs in a teaspoon of grainy mustard. Madame Bernard makes her own garni and doubles the number of vegetables.

The meat and fruit combination might not appeal at first sight. The first taste should convince you.

SURREAL SOIRÉE

"ALISTAIR. Problem."

The neighbours have problems like other people have coffee – a couple of large ones first thing in the morning and two or three more during the day. Oil leaks and scarlet fever, vets' bills and bad backs, mobiles lost in cement-mixers, reluctantly pregnant girlfriends, cats killing the canaries. I could help with some of them, but not with others.

At first hearing this problem didn't sound too demanding. Lola was having some specially invited guests one evening in June. It seemed that Rico and the boys would be away with the horses. She needed a man for the night, would I be available?

"What is it?" I asked, "A kind of party?"

"More of a *soirée*," she replied.

I imagined being something between a host and an escort; helping with the drinks and being charming to guests. This was the sort of problem I liked.

As things worked out, I was faced with a mad dash back from England to fulfil my June engagement. Driving through the night, I arrived in the village in the early hours of that Saturday morning. If I could just have ten hours' solid sleep everything would be fine for the *soirée*.

A couple of hours later Djojo was banging on the gate.

"I knew you wouldn't forget!" he shouted, "Everyone said you weren't coming, but I knew you would keep a promise."

"I didn't forget – but right now I need sleep, Djojo. Tell your *maman* not to worry, I will be there tonight."

"No – you have to come now," he said. "Mama needs you in the village hall before 8 o'clock."

I groaned, swallowed a mug of black coffee and made my way down to the hall. The first people I saw were Rico and his sons. Their trip was cancelled and I need not have rushed back; Lola

SURREAL SOIRÉE

had hosts and escorts aplenty. She was in complete control as usual, the husky foghorn commanding and cajoling. I was given a couple of things to do straight away – yawns, trembling hands, bloodshot eyes or not.

First I had to encircle concrete pillars with wire, laurel leaves and flowers; a job I'm spectacularly unsuited for, even at my best. When I finished the effect was a mix of Roman orgy and Mae West's boudoir. Lola was very impressed. Next I had to tape black paper over all the hall windows. I finished as quickly as I could, thinking there must be a film or slide show as part of the *soirée*. Lack of sleep robs me of good humour and vocabulary, or I might have asked a few more questions and the evening would not have held its surprises.

Outside in the courtyard, Rico was putting together a makeshift bar in one corner, complete with more leaves and flowers. A mobile disco was going up on the terrace. Some *soirée*. I pleaded exhaustion and Lola said she would see me later.

"Do you still need me?" I asked.

"Come anyway," she winked and poked my ribs. "You might see something you like…"

Too tired to care about the innuendo, I went for a long siesta and dreamt of Mae West.

In the evening I had a quick strip wash and found some uncreased clothes. On my way to the *soirée* I passed the sisters-in-law and friends, enjoying the late sun under the mulberry tree. They asked what the activity was in the village hall, and I told them all I knew – which wasn't much.

At the doors I barely recognised Rico. A jeans and T-shirt man if ever there was, he stood tugging at a stiff shirt-collar and wearing a new grey suit, 5% wool 95% cardboard. He wouldn't have looked more uncomfortable in a leotard and skates. The expression on my face must have been incredulous. As he caught my eye, he lifted his arms helplessly like a tired seagull, as if to say, "What can I do? She made me wear it." He was collecting tickets from arriving guests and making a brave effort to be suave. The DIY tattoos didn't help.

I didn't need a ticket and went through into the courtyard.

EN GARD

Rows of chairs had been arranged in a semicircle. Leading down the hall steps and in front of the chairs was a roll of red carpet. The mobile disco was playing something soothing as people took their seats, and spotlights were trained on the side doors of the hall. The chairs were filling up quickly and more cars were still arriving. The sisters-in-law were at the main door, with husbands and assorted friends, but without tickets. Rico was thrown into a flap. To turn away the elderly backbone of the village would be a blunder, but something was making him reluctant to let them in. As usual Lola made the decision, and the old folk took some seats in the front row. I slipped into the back row, genuinely puzzled, just as a chill North wind began to blow.

The music stopped and Lola tested her microphone. She was drenched, not dripping, with gypsy gold, in full battle make-up, mini-skirt and stilettoes. A flashing smile welcomed us all to the *soirée*.

"Have you all received your order forms?" she asked.

Most of the crowd waved sheets of paper in the air. I thought "Order forms...?"

"Good. I hope you will all enjoy the show tonight," Lola went on, "Afterwards there will be some refreshments and I will be available to answer any questions. One last thing, ladies and gentlemen, no photography please."

Show? Questions? Photography?

"And now," Lola nodded to Rico who opened the side doors. "And now, ladies and gentlemen, this ensemble is available in pink, red, turquoise and, of course, white. Please welcome Marie-Jo!"

Through the door and into the bright lights stepped Marie-Jo, a leggy blonde in a pair of tiny lace briefs and matching bra. The music began, with lots of back-beat, and she twirled flashily before slinking down the steps and along the carpet in front of the chairs. The old folk sat forward in their seats. She twirled a few more times and, on the return trip, she stopped, hands on hips, to give the sisters-in-law a good view. They looked at one another and nodded enthusiastically. She smiled and then she was gone.

It had been surreal. Along with Dali's melting watch, and

SURREAL SOIRÉE

Magritte's bowler hat, we had Lola's open-air *soirée* in sleepy rural France. I'd worked in Soho for seven years, and had seen more strangers' flesh in the last seven minutes than I ever saw there. I closed my eyes. My God, I thought, what are the old folk going to make of this? They were staunch Protestants, regular chapel-goers, teetotal and very proper. This must seem like Sodom and Gomorrah. But I underestimated them. As I watched they seemed to be enjoying every second.

Marie-Jo was followed by Michelle in a G-string and bra. This time there was an audible response – some light clapping and *'mais ouis'* and scribbling on the order forms. The wind was picking up and I thought how typical of Lola's luck to choose the only cold evening between April and November. The models were tanned, but going blue, with goose bumps and nipples erect. They kept moving and smiling, warming to their audience if nothing else.

"The next ensemble is available only in black or white. It is for the generous figure – please welcome Janine!"

The doors were flung open and Janine appeared. A touch under five feet, with classic child-bearing hips, sturdy agricultural limbs, big red hands and broad splayed feet. My father would have said that she wouldn't blow over in a strong wind. Just as well under these conditions. She didn't bat an eyelid. She marched proudly down the steps with her shimmering folds of dimpled flesh, to defend everyone's right to wear a G-string. There was wild applause.

Each girl made the catwalk seven or eight times, the blacked out windows giving them their changing-room. As it got colder and colder, they marched faster and faster. The audience wasn't dressed for the unexpected wind, but the models were suffering through the smiles. The *soirée* ended with a wedding trousseau in embroidered silk, complete with white stockings and garters.

I couldn't get an idea out of my head. If Sandy and I had arrived in the village for the first time tonight, what, might we have wondered, did they do behind closed doors?

Drinks were served to keep out the cold, while order forms were collected. I went home to get a sweater and passed the sisters-in-law back on their bench. They asked me what I thought.

"Excellent," I said. "I spent a fortune."

"Did you?" said one of them, well into her eighties. "Hope you didn't buy anything for me!"

And they all fell about laughing.

Later, Lola told me one old lady had placed an order for G-strings. It's a difficult image to dispel when we meet in the baker's.

A ROOF OVER OUR HEADS

MY BROTHER, Ian, and his wife Ann wrote to ask if they could visit in June. It would be good to see them and their reaction to the house. We explained how primitive things were – chemical loo, solar shower in the courtyard, camping-gaz – and they agreed it would be better to book into a local *gîte*. We could shower there, too. Sandy was still working back in England and she would be around for the beginning and end of their stay. I was planning to attack my first roof to coincide with their 'holiday'. It would be good to have a helping hand and a second opinion.

The roof was 20 feet long, 17 feet at its widest, tapering to eight. Three pine trunks served as the main beams along its length and nailed to these, at right angles, and mortared into the back walls, were twenty-four battens. The battens were split chestnut. Ancient canal tiles were laid concave side down between the battens, and another row of tiles concave side up covered the battens from above. A roof like this is Roman, unchanged in principle for two thousand years. We planned to save and recycle as many tiles as we could – not only because the colours were beautiful, and the lichen on them added to this, but also because to replace them would be prohibitive. Battens would be renewed with pressure-treated wood and the old ones would be cut up, to be stored as firewood. Two of the three major beams needed to be replaced. They were insect-ridden and rotten from years of neglect. Even in this condition they were long and heavy enough to be battering-rams and giant levers and my main worry was how to get them down safely. Adding to the problem, the front of this outbuilding was made up of wooden doors and windows. These had sagged and warped under the weight of the failing roof. They were now doing the work of the lowest beam, keeping the roof from collapsing. Ian and Ann could not arrive soon enough.

But before they came I needed to clear away years of agricul-

EN GARD

tural rubbish, take down a mezzanine floor, prune the rusty wire holding everything together, and find a solid floor to work from. I began by dismantling an old cow byre and used the spokes from it to hammer into the earth, trying to find its depth. They disappeared for all of their 2 feet length without hitting rock-bottom. One job seemed to create another. I bought a pickaxe, a shovel and fifty rubble bags and set to work.

Moist on top, the soil underneath was compacted and liberally mixed with sheep droppings. This building and the ground-floor rooms of the house had been used to keep sheep and goats, so it wasn't surprising. But the pungency and irritant power of 50 years of desiccated shit was overwhelming. I laboured, sneezed, coughed and scratched my way through 350 bags of it, and no matter how many solar showers and shampoos I took, I hummed for weeks. As the postmistress dropped off Sandy's daily postcards, I could tell she wanted to ask, '"Monsieur Scott, what IS that smell?" but she was too polite.

From the 350 bags I sprinkled some of the priceless manure on our plot of land opposite, which one day might produce tomatoes like pumpkins, and pumpkins like cartwheels. The rest I made available to anyone who wanted it. The remaining sacks went up to the local dump. On my recent trips up there, I've noticed the wild flowers are breathtaking.

Meanwhile, it was a preoccupation that neither Sandy nor I had any idea where to find two tree trunks to replace the old ones.

"We need a Yellow Pages," Sandy said, 'for timber merchants." Not having a phone meant no directories for us and the neighbours had used theirs to light barbecues.

"While we're in town, I'll ask in a bar if we can use their directory," said Sandy.

Luck was on our side, however. Next day we were in what passes for a traffic jam here – four or five cars held up for a moment or two. Heading the congestion was a lorry, loaded with exactly what we were looking for. As the traffic moved off, I said to Sandy,

"I'm going to follow that lot. We need to know where we can buy those beams."

"Good idea, Scotty, unless they're going to Spain......"

A ROOF OVER OUR HEADS

The lorry was not heading for Spain. It pulled into a side road leading to a builders' merchant where several hundred beams stood piled into various lengths and diameters. There were also battens ready-cut, square or triangular. Problem solved. These materials might be exotic or uncalled for at B&Q in England, but hereabouts they are everyday and everywhere. We ordered what we needed and arranged a day and time for delivery.

In practice, the date meant something, the time didn't – but no better or worse than waiting in all day for the gas man in England. The driver unloaded two giant beams and thirty battens in the street outside the gates. He created a show-jumping fence in seconds. It would take time and effort to dismantle it. I called on two sons from next door to help move the wood into the courtyard. We made up slings from rope to act as handholds and moved the telegraph poles a foot at a time. The French proverb *'Petit, petit, l'oiseau fait son nid'* (little by little the bird makes his nest) seemed pretty apt.

THE WORK CREW ARRIVES

"RIGHT, OUR KID, let's have a look at this 'ouse, then," said Ian as we waited for luggage at Nimes airport. He sounded very Yorkshire. He was laid-back and enthusiastic at once. I felt I needed to warn him to be prepared for a bit of a shock.

" – but it's not as bad as it looks. Better not tell the Duchess though, it might be too much for her heart."

We stopped off in Uzès for lunch and for them to sample the cafè-terrace life.

"Oh, yes," Ann kept saying, "oh, yes."

We drove to the house and their first view through the gates. Ann was very quiet for a while, and then said, 'Oh, yes."

Ian said, "By heck."

We did the tour and it was like having someone look through my underwear drawer. At its end I said,

"Well, what do you think?'

"Oh, yes," said Ann seeing the finished article in her head, but big brother was less enthusiastic.

"You've got some bloody arsehole taking this on. I wouldn't 'ave. Not with all these bloody roofs to do."

I wondered what he'd say when I told him that was exactly what we were going to do, and what he'd say when we'd done it. I broke the news.

"Which case are my work clothes in, luv?" he asked Ann. Bless his heart, he would have started right away.

"Tomorrow, mate," I said. "Tomorrow."

I warmed the casserole for supper, and everyone agreed that an early night before an early start might be a good idea. I offered to walk them back to the *gîte*. We did not get very far. We turned left past Rico and Lola's place. They had waited up to say hello, and to welcome Ian and Ann to France. I thought it was wonderful. They called us up for a glass or two. Lola had bought expensive wine, not their usual six bottles for 10 euros. It was gone midnight when we staggered out. Ian loved the pastis, and Rico taught him all the French he thought he might need, *'ça va?'*, 'Rico', ' Pastis'.

Ian's first morning on the job set the pattern for the rest of his stay.

"Cup of tea?" I'd ask.

"Go on, then," and he'd wander outside to look at the day's workload.

I suggested a way to dismantle the roof from tiles through to beams and by the time I'd washed up our cups, he already had a pile of tiles at the foot of his ladder. With Ann and Sandy, we formed a chain gang, taking tiles off, passing them down, storing and stacking them in what might one day be the kitchen. Twenty minutes into this, Ian noticed a lot of the tiles had been cut or shaped at the widest end, so many and so well done, that it couldn't be accidental breakage.

"Don't know what this is all about," he said, "but we ought to stack these buggers separately."

As the temperature rose and Ian put on his denim pork-pie hat, it occurred to me that between the tiles would be a nice warm place for scorpions to live.

"Give over, you daft sod," he scoffed, "there's no scorpions in France." So naturally, a couple of minutes later the first scorpion, about the size of a cigarette, landed on his head and slid onto his arm.

"Bloody hell!" from the top of the ladder. "There *are* scorpions in France, you know! Tread on the little blighter!" and he flicked it to the ground.

As it got hotter, and we grew tired, the vocabulary dropped off to six or seven words as tiles passed from hand to hand. 'Scorpion', 'Big spider', 'Little spider', or, of particular tiles, 'Heavy bastard'.

At the final count there were 700 whole tiles, and 150 shaped or broken ones. The colours ranged from wet sand to baby pink to dull brick, and more than half were beautifully speckled with lichen – mustard yellow, emerald and turquoise. The animal tally was seven scorpions, and three dozen spiders. All the lizards had scuttled away and watched us indignantly from the walls. Another significant number was 40. Degrees centigrade. We all needed to drink lots of water and get into the shade.

You don't usually take a siesta in Yorkshire, and Ian saw no reason to take on foreign ways. Instead he set about the mortar on the back wall with hammer and chisel, to free the battens ready for removal. It was sand-rich and as crumbly as digestive biscuit and it came down easily enough.

"We'll need a better mix than that," Ian said as we bagged up the debris. Never having mixed mortar in my life I muttered,

"Something else to learn in a hurry."

"You what?" Ian asked.

"Nothing, mate." I replied. Best if he didn't know how woeful my knowledge was.

"Anyhow, that's a good day's graft," he said. "Let's 'ave a pastis." His second day in France, and he didn't seem to be missing his Tetley's Bitter one bit.

"Now then, about those beams..."

"Tomorrow, mate. Tomorrow."

Over the second pastis, the wasps arrived. A small cloud of them, and Gabby, on a visit, told us they were wood-boring wasps; a colony on the look out for a new home. We should take care, he counselled, because they could be aggressive when on the move, and the sooner we called the fire brigade to come and deal with them the better.

"Give over," said Ian, when I'd translated. "Cut down some of them fig branches and give us them 'ere."

He lit a fire under the wasps, and when there was heat in the fire, he piled on the green fig cuttings. In minutes, Claude and Catherine coughed as they passed on their promenade, and the wasps left to find a home less polluted. Wasps, it seemed, didn't like a smart arse from Yorkshire. I did.

Overnight, Ian had come up with a solution for dealing with the beams, without bringing down the walls, or killing ourselves.

"Cup of tea?"

"Go on, then."

While I made tea, Ian started to make props from some of the

THE WORK CREW ARRIVES

battens we had bought and some old door timbers. Nailed into a crude 'Y' shape they would support the beams while we cut through them in manageable chunks. We laid some planks against the warped wooden facade for bits of beam to bounce off or roll down. If they fell anywhere else it would be reasonably safe.

"*Allez!*" said Ian. The fourth French word he had learned.

It worked. We never felt out of control of the huge weights, despite our primitive tools. It was all much easier to do than imagine and worry about. We waggled one stump out of the wall and tossed it caber-style clear of the ladder. Ian checked the surrounding wall for damage, and found an old pickaxe blade that had been used to spread the weight of the beam in the wall. We moved to the other end for the second stump. When he checked the wall this time, he found something completely different.

Not the *'cache d'or'* (the hidden gold) that our neighbours had convinced us was somewhere in the house. But treasure of a kind. Beyond the hole where the beam had sat was another hole that someone had taken particular care to make. Forgetting scorpions, Ian plunged his hand into the space and came up with a bundle of paper, some torn into scraps but some whole sheets amongst them.

"Look at this, Al," he said. "I think they're old letters." There were several handfuls, a few still in their envelopes, all badly damp-stained, dating from the years immediately after the war.

I grabbed a biscuit tin from the garage, emptied out the curry spices, and filled it with the letters.

Reading faded ink in a stranger's handwriting in a foreign language didn't reveal very much at first sight. I hoped they were love letters or full of old secrets. They would have to wait for Sandy, with a magnifying glass and our heavyweight dictionary. Perhaps we could take them round to Madame Bernard. She was our village granny and also our local historian. I imagined the glee on her face at the prospect of ancient gossip.

With a good system, now tried and tested, the second beam required us to alter the lengths of the props and follow the same routine. It all went sweetly and was quick.

"Getting those beams down is one thing. Getting the new buggers back up is summat else. Pastis, our kid?"

Madame Bernard accepted the biscuit tin at her front door and listened as we explained how and where the letters were found. She opened the tin in the street in her haste and was mystified by the smell of the Indian spices. We explained that, too.

For four or five days, whenever she was not making her famous soups, or chatting idly with her friends around the visiting meat, fish or vegetable vans, she trawled through the letters and the torn scraps. She shared the letters with the third-agers on the bench in the early evenings, the better to remember the tiny details.

She knew everyone mentioned in the letters by name, but found nothing forbidden or lascivious. Instead she found a snapshot of things important to a village family, immediately after the last war. The letters were to and from J G, conscripted and serving in Montpellier. They talked of a weekend pass, and when he might arrive, of his billet and the fever that kept him in bed for a week. For him, there was the information that the Ekel family had started to harvest the pearl barley too early, despite being counselled against it; that a neighbour had bought two more goats; the possibility of renting extra land in nearby Lussan. Someone had forgotten to post his banns and his wedding could not go ahead as planned. There were murmurings that another in the village was making too much of her misery in her pregnancy.

The real poignancy lay in the superstition behind the hiding of the letters in the first place. It was felt that if family letters were hidden in the house, the family would never again be split, and the house would be theirs forever. It hadn't worked out that way.

A WEEKEND AT THE RACES

RIGHT ON CUE for the pastis, Rico arrived, but not his usual, cheerful self.

"Alistair. *Voitures. Cheveux. Problème.*" he said. "Alistair. Cars. Horses. Problem." No verbs. From experience, I knew this was something serious. As he went on, we realised that we were going to have a break from roofing and it somehow involved horses and mountains and the whole weekend.

Rico's main source of income in those days was breeding and training pure-bred Arab horses for endurance races. This is roughly the same as point-to-pointing in the U.K. There was an important 90 kilometres race in the Cevennes at the weekend and one of his support vehicles had broken down. This is where we came in. He needed both us, and the rented Peugeot 206 I had while the campervan was under repair, to be the support team for his second horse. As Ian and Ann were on holiday it seemed right for them to decide – and bravely, without knowing exactly what was involved, they shouted together,

"We'll do it!"

The next day, Friday, and still unsure what support teams do, we set off at midday in the Peugeot, following Rico in his overloaded 4x4 with horsebox in tow. The Arab geldings inside, Othello and Thor, were skittish and highly-strung and seemed in danger of harming themselves as they kicked against the inside of their boxes.

The far side of Ales was uncharted territory to me and we were soon in the foothills of the Cevennes. It was a vast landscape, magnificent and wild, row upon row of forested mountains fading into paler grey-green. Granite outcrops broke through the trees and birds of prey cruised high overhead. There was no sign of a human hand anywhere, other than the road we were on. The North Yorkshire moors shrank to tame backyards by comparison.

EN GARD

In the early evening we arrived at base camp. This was nothing more than a field on a hillside, part of a distant equestrian centre. The horses were unloaded into warm, dry, cosy stables at the centre. We were to sleep in the field. After we'd put up tents and unrolled musty sleeping bags, Rico took us off to the stables where he introduced us to other competitors and friends. Not wanting anyone to know that he had a team of complete amateurs helping him, he introduced us as experts from Newmarket who could not speak or understand French. He hoped that no-one else spoke English or would try and interrogate us about bloodstock and sale prices.

We ate frugally. The flies put Ann off, the vague idea that it might be horse-meat put Ian off and I was just too tired. We slept fitfully in damp bedding on a sloping hillside of unforgiving ground and awoke the next morning unfit in every way for whatever was expected of us. Coffee was in meagre rations. I need lots of it early in the day. While I was drinking my small cup, Rico arrived to finally tell us what would be going on. He took me to one side with a map and directions for the route of the race. The idea of endurance racing is that the strength and fitness of the horse is tested. There are regular veterinary checks and stops for water and food at special stations on the course. It would be our job to make sure fresh food and water arrived at these stations ahead of the horse. Riding over the finishing line did not necessarily signify the winner. The subsequent assessment of the horse's condition counted for everything – food and water was vital. It was an onerous responsibility for a team of rank amateurs. When I got back to my coffee it was cold and the field kitchen was packed up.

Horse-feed and containers of water were piled into the Peugeot boot, and onto any space on the back seat. At the pre-race vet inspection, Rico was as nervous as a football manager on a Saturday afternoon.

Seventy horses started. They were going across country and the support vehicles were sticking to the roads. There was a scramble among the cars and 4x4s like the start of a Grand Prix of old as we set off towards the first station. We fought our corner in getting

A WEEKEND AT THE RACES

water to our horse and rider, spraying and sponging them both to keep them cool. Owners, trainers and riders compared notes and then we were off again. It seemed simple enough and we began to relax a little...

At the next station Rico was called aside. One of his horses had lost a shoe and gone lame. The rider, his son Toni, needed help. Tell a gypsy that his son and his horse are in trouble at the same time and he becomes unhinged. Without saying anything to us, Rico shot off in the 4x4. Bewildered, we set off after him.

After a few miles, Ann wondered out loud

"Is this a good idea? Should we be following Rico? Djimmy is still in the race after all." She was right. We turned back. At the last rest station, the support vehicles were long gone and we now had to rely on the map and the directions to get us to the next stop. We took a wrong turn down a dirt track and lost valuable time. I put my foot down and the little car had all four wheels off the ground over the bumps. We missed the next station. It was all going horribly wrong. But we got to the one after that with time to spare. This was a vets' inspection point as well as a food stop. We had to check Othello's heart rate and coax it down to 55 beats per minute. We sponged him and he drank deeply and nibbled at some food. The missed station hadn't done him any harm, and the vet passed him fit to continue.

Lunchtime was spent re-stocking the car for the afternoon session. We were hungry enough to consider some of the dried oats ourselves. As well as hungry, we were hot and sunburned.

"In the mountains, you're closer to the sun," Ian said, and managed to make it sound very profound.

Just after five o'clock Djimmy brought Othello home in second place. The first horse over the line was disqualified by the vets and so a team of complete amateurs had supported the eventual winner.

"What now?" I asked Rico.

"Now his value goes up. Maybe someone rich from the Emirates will take an interest in him," he said dreamily.

"What do WE do now, I mean?"

"We pack up and go home."

EN GARD

Back at the garage, Rico handed Ian and Ann the rosette that Othello had won, and said,
"Not bad for your first time."
"That's high praise from Rico," I said, 'believe me."
"You don't get this on a bloody package deal to Costa del Sol," Ian said, stifling a yawn.
We finished our spaghetti and our cheap Côtes du Rhône and thought roofing a doddle after all.

CAFÉ MOMENTS

EARLY ON SUNDAY morning, we cut the beams to length. We tried to lift them and could not.

We wanted some thinking time – what we came to call 'café-moments'. The three of us would find a bar with tables in the sun, order coffee and stare into space. Each of us like a dog with a bone, chewing over a problem as it arose. There was something about the to-ing and fro-ing of the people in the street, the soft hum of conversation at other tables, that relaxed the mind wonderfully. Like watching tropical fish, languid in their tank. Sometimes synapses would pop, and solutions appeared out of mid-air.

"It's the alpha waves," said Ann.

As the coffee froth dried in the cups, Ian said, "We'll cut the buggers in half."

At first I couldn't see the value in a beam that would not span the walls, and then it dawned.

"Along its length!"

I could see three problems at once. Would the beam be strong enough, cut down its centre? How long might it take to cut it with a handsaw? And finally, if we were to cut it with a petrol chain saw, how on earth could I justify the expense?

Even on a Sunday in France, dedicated to deep and quiet pleasures – promenading and eating mostly – we were to answer all three questions. Stopping in a nearby village, we lingered near the old wash-house. A pair of stone baths big enough to swallow up the dirty clothes of the whole village – one for rinsing, and one for washing, and a stone gargoyle spewing spring water into the first.

"If walls could talk!" said Ann, thinking of all the things that must have been aired here besides clothes, as women down the centuries did their smalls.

"Never mind that," said Ian, "look at them beams in t' roof." The beams were ancient, long and cut down their centres.

EN GARD

Back at the courtyard, Ian said, "Go on, then" to the idea of a cup of tea. He made a start on the beam with the handsaw. While the kettle boiled, I explained to Ann that the neighbours had never seen a kettle before, and didn't believe that we boiled water in it for tea and coffee, instead of using a small saucepan.

"It'll take two weeks!" shouted Ian from one end of a beam. He had spent five minutes sawing on a beam-end and had only cut a nick in it.

"Twenty minutes on, twenty minutes off for two bloody weeks. Sod that for a game of soldiers."

Rico came by to tell us that the lame horse was much better, and tea gave way to pastis. He screwed up his face at the first taste.

"Alistair! Its not good, the pastis!"

"It's '51'," I said, "it's what we always drink."

"Wait there," he said on his way out of the garage.

Five minutes later, two of his sons carried a rusty, half-sized fridge into the garage.

"That's no good to me – I don't have electricity," I said.

"Yes you do," said Rico coming into the garage, and letting out a few more feet of electric cable from a coil over his shoulder. "The other end is wired into my kitchen."

Inside the fridge were two recycled plastic water bottles – half ice, half water.

"At last I can get a decent pastis in an Englishman's home."

"And," said Ann, "we can cut the beams with a chainsaw. The electric ones are a third of the price of the petrol jobbies – on special offer at Mr Bricolage."

"Do women ever stop shopping?" I asked. She'd really earned her fish pie, and I put it on to warm.

At 9.30 the next morning I was the owner of the chainsaw that Ann had scouted for. By ten, we were cutting the beam and by two it was done. It was to be the only sophisticated tool we were to use in getting the new beams into place. Other than that, it was ropes, pulleys, levers, elbow grease and good luck. Using a nearby tree and the original sound beam, and with one end of the new beam in a rope sling we hoisted it above its slot in the wall. The opposite end we raised with levers and the 'Y' props. This left us three

CAFÉ MOMENTS

feet below the hole. I put up a ladder and hooked my arm under the beam. It felt secure enough, and a good lifting position and I fancied my chances to lift and jerk the beam home. I told Ian my plan.

"Go on, then."

I puffed and paced, and did it again like a Bulgarian weightlifter at the Olympics. I huffed carbon dioxide from my lungs, and sucked in oxygen in its place, climbed the ladder, got comfortable, hooked my arm under the beam and lifted. It was easy. The sling allowed the whole thing to move smoothly into place. I could hear clapping. I accepted the praise a bit dishonestly. Fear gives strength, no doubt, but actually we had stumbled on a good system. Anxious not to lose momentum, we cracked on with the second beam. After days of apprehension we'd finished this part of the job in 90 minutes. Using a long length of timber and a spirit level, we made sure the beams were level and mortared them into place. Then we rested on our laurels.

The next day, with the morning tea ceremony over, Ian had mocked up a section of roof on the courtyard floor. We calculated optimum spacing for the battens so that the tiles would sit well. We measured time and time again at roof level, and again at floor level. '"Measure twice, cut once," our father had coached us. Things have moved on since those days, Dad. Measure as many times as you want, until it becomes procrastination.

We spent a mindless hour flattening off the points of three hundred six-inch nails, to avoid splitting the new battens. We passed battens up to the roof, filled our pockets with nails and started. Ian was top-side of the roof, and I was below him. I would feed a batten to him, he would measure the gap say "yes", and wait for me. I would measure the gap for the bottom of the roof, say "yes" and we hammered. Batten, measure, "yes" and hammer. Batten, measure, "yes" and hammer. I don't suppose it took us two hours, and that because we are our father's sons; halfway through we stopped and measured and measured again. "They fuck you up your mum and dad," as Philip Larkin said.

It was as much as Ian and Ann could do in helping with the roof. Their holiday was over. It made Ian smile to think that when people asked what he had done on holiday, he could say, "I built a roof in the south of France."

I was on my own at the house. Sandy had gone back to England just after Ian and Ann. There was just the small matter of 700 plus tiles to go back on the roof. A big, heavy jigsaw puzzle 15ft in the air. The girls had cleaned the tiles as they stacked them – Sandy meticulously sorting them by colour and lichen pattern. I had forgotten just how heavy they were. Going backwards and forwards, up and down the ladder, I found I could safely carry four at a time. Only two hundred and twelve trips, then. A cycle racing team in skintight lycra stopped for a breather outside the gates.

"I'll have legs like yours in about three days," I thought.

All the tiles went up. Those that needed to be mortared in were mortared in, and then I found one more reason to thank big brother. The shaped tiles that had intrigued him enough to suggest that they be stacked separately, turned out to be the ones that finished the leading edge of the tapering roof. The rest simply laid one on top of the other, curve up or curve down. God help any cat that tries to move them in pursuit of amorous adventure!

And my legs did improve.

Pride comes before a fall.

Full of my roofing self now, I decided to tackle another, smaller roof before I had to go back to England. It joined the finished roof onto the main house. It covered a summer kitchen. A space for cooking *al fresco* in the hottest months. Ours had two ancient stone sinks in it and nothing else. This little roof had been re-done recently – but badly, using flat modern tiles. They had to go. It came apart quickly and easily. Having no interest in the tiles, I threw them to the ground to smash, rather than carry them down. Standing on the lowest beam, I started to lever and hammer off the battens. I threw them to the ground, too. The last of them was reluctant to shift. I repositioned myself to give it a serious clout.

There was a sharp crack to my right and the beam gave way. I was eight feet off the ground and I fell heavily on my right side. My buttock took the brunt of the fall. My ribs and my elbow felt damaged, too. I lay still, to get my wind back. To my right was the

CAFÉ MOMENTS

treacherous beam – sound for all its exposed length, but rotted to sawdust where it had been in the wall. To my left, inches away, was the pile of battens that I had tossed down, their six-inch nails pointing upwards. They would have made an awful mess of me; a big, bloody kebab.

I thanked the patron saint of roofers and begged forgiveness for being cocky about roofing. I still had much to learn and, if I was much more careful, I hoped I might live to do so.

A HAT-TRICK OF ROOFS

SANDY WAS BACK for the last bit of roof left to do, before the weather got too hot. It covered her 'studio', was closest to the road, in full view of the village. I felt under pressure and scrutiny to do it just right. It was twice the size of the first roof, and at twice the height. It had an apex with an unusual beam. This was in good condition and I saw no reason to replace it. But it was a chestnut trunk of gnarled and irregular girth and I knew that the battens would not sit evenly on its contours. We invested in some cheap and cheerful scaffolding to take down 1,800 tiles. At the end of this, Sandy's hands would be so rough and coarse that, even by winter, she wouldn't be able to put on tights without using surgical gloves.

Only one beam had to come down using the Scott Brothers' patent method. But being higher, longer and heavier than before, this time the cut lengths bounced alarmingly against ladders, props and scaffold. Getting the new beam back up required a café moment or two. I decided that pastis and machismo might do the job.

One early evening I suggested to the men in Rico's family that it was not possible for any man to lift my beam into place. I provoked enough indignation to get things going. From inception to final planning took an hour and five pastis.

Two of us went up ladders and sat on the wall to receive the beam. The others clutched the beam to their chests, and synchronised each step up their ladders. Eighteen inches from the top of the wall and it was time to launch the beam towards its final resting place. It was a splendid effort, and unfortunate that it landed on my thigh, pinning me down. "Between a rock and a hard thing," I thought as granite bit into my leg. I swore in two languages. The boys moved like lightning to set me free.

There were ten days of bad temper and frustration then as the

A HAT-TRICK OF ROOFS

temperature began to climb and nothing went smoothly. Perhaps we'd overdosed on roofs. Plumbing suddenly seemed exciting and attractive. We needed lots of spacers to accommodate the old beam's oddities, and then we discovered that the walls at each end were of variable thicknesses, which threw out the positions of the last tiles. More by luck than judgement we juggled a solution.

"Alistair," a visiting Canadian called from the road, "it's crooked."

"Nature abhors a straight bloody line," I answered. She didn't deserve that.

Almost immediately, a village mason stopped by on his bike. He had given up working in the heat.

"*Un petit conseil,*" he offered. A little advice. A trade secret, perhaps.

"The first tile should be a broken tile. Then all the other tiles will sit better."

We thanked him, of course. Little did he know we were about to go round and do that to each row. We'd found out by trial and error, like we'd found out most things about roofs.

MADAME BERNARD'S SOUP

MY GRANDPARENTS would have liked it here; the house and the village. They were from tamer English countryside on the Bedfordshire/Cambridgeshire borders, from villages a few miles apart. A farmer's son and a publican's daughter, who met 'in service' as a blacksmith and a downstairs maid. They courted in a rose garden, where servants were allowed to walk on Sunday afternoons, and married before my grandfather went off to war. The farm was still in his family when my mother was a young woman. There is a photo of her, with her sister and assorted cousins and step-cousins and half-cousins, in a hay-cart, with pitchforks and headscarves and a black and white dog. They are having the time of their lives.

'The country' was a weekend jaunt in my mother's childhood. The four of them packed into a motorbike and sidecar, visiting relations. Coming home with a couple of pheasants or gooseberries grown to the size of walnuts by 'night soil'. My grandparents' dream was to retire there, but they never did. 'The country' had changed so much there was really nowhere for them to retire to. So many things had changed, between their childhoods and mine, that talk of harvest supper and mole-catchers meant nothing to me. I didn't know they were a link to a disappearing world. After they died I regretted that I hadn't listened harder and asked more questions. I might be a better pastry-maker if I had.

Madame Bernard is our adopted grandparent here in the village. She is the universal granny, favouring cardigans and cotton aprons on which she wipes floury hands. A humble, independent woman with strong ideas about right and wrong; a willow and an oak. On winter nights she is the only sign of life on the streets, collecting logs from her woodpile. On summer evenings she sits under the mulberry tree with her sisters-in-law; still plenty to talk about after all these years. She lives alone in a house opposite the

MADAME BERNARD'S SOUP

clock tower, which may account for her slight deafness. The clock chimes the hours twice with long metallic drips, and 80 years is a lot of hours. It was her parents' house and she remembers her father laying the kitchen floor when she was seven. We have the same patterned tiles in our house and have dated them from her memory.

I have been no further inside her house than her kitchen, where she spends most of her time, and where she produces her soup. She eats lightly. Soft sucking fruits like ripe peaches and pears that don't need a lot of work; some boiled fish, and her soup. A vegetable broth that is her staff of life, winter and summer. It uses up the outside leaves of cabbages and celery tops. She makes her own pistou and her own stock from butcher's bones. Her kitchen smells like a link to that disappearing world, and this time I've made sure I listen and ask the right questions.

As well as a link to the past, the smell of her soup will always be a memory of the autumn floods, two years ago; one of the better memories.

August had given way to September, and our days of work, rest and play melded into one another. We didn't notice the subtle changes in the weather, summer to autumn. One day the horses in the field opposite were skittish and dogs howled with their tails between their legs, sniffing something in the air.

Slowly the sky turned a dirty sulphurous yellow, and the egg-white on aluminium tang of ozone filled our noses too. Air pressure dropped. We were in for a storm, and like good sailors we made ready – putting away tools and cement mixer, and taking jeans from the line.

But the rain didn't come. First we had a dry storm of thunder and lightning. The valley is a natural Albert Hall, and the noise filled all the empty spaces in our skulls, the flashes crackling like cold bacon in hot fat. Surges of electric current switched the stereo on and off like a poltergeist. Violent gusts of wind rattled the fig tree, bending branches to the ground; it tossed buckets against courtyard walls and our heavy iron gates opened and slammed shut.

The wind died in the afternoon and the sky began to boil. When

EN GARD

the rain started it was like a black velvet purse had been opened and a pile of old pennies tipped out, so dark and noisy were the clouds and the drops of water. Big sploshes that stung our skin soon turned to a wall of water, the other side of the courtyard lost in the downpour.

We had been caught in Gardoise rain before, out in the van. A flash flood in the mountains, short-lived but powerful enough to turn the road red with mud, like a slit artery. Solid and heavy lump that we were, it threatened to lift us up and carry us off in the current. We felt a few notches safer in the house.

In blissful ignorance, we settled ourselves down to read between the power cuts. There was some cake, though no ale, and we were warm and dry and used to wet sieges on the boat. We wished we had miners' helmets for when the lights went out, and that we knew a couple of people who could play mah-jong. We have lost whole days to mah-jong, a good bad weather game. I once won with a 'Hand of Heaven', which scores 'Infinity' – even in a suburban dining room.

"So, what we need," said Sandy, "are two Chinese coal miners looking for shelter from the storm."

"Or two Cornish tin miners with spare helmets and some pasties in their lunchbox – we can soon teach them how to play."

We made tea and did rain-checks as night fell.

"I think it's easing off – I can see the fig tree."

My damp pillow woke me around first light, and I stepped out of bed into a puddle. Hours of driving rain had found its way in, as water always does, through any cracks and holes. Opening the doors I could see the rain was as strong as ever, and we had a river in the courtyard. I have never seen the Irrawaddy, but in my imagination it is a wide toffee slab of water full of water buffalo and floating vegetation, swirling round big bends. Minus the water buffalo, that was what we had streaming under our gates. Banging against the inside of the gates were a plastic bowl and scrubbing brush, a flip-flop and about a ton of tangled grass and weeds. As the rain fell the water table rose and spontaneous springs appeared in the bedrock. We were lucky – elsewhere these springs erupted through house floors.

MADAME BERNARD'S SOUP

"Do you think it's safe to go out?" Sandy asked.

"The water's moving quite fast in the lane, but I don't think it's too deep. If we can stay on our feet we should be OK. We could make it to the baker's."

We had some wet weather gear from the boat, and cursed ourselves for not bringing our sailing wellies. We had thought we wouldn't need them, moving to the south of France. Wrapped up like mackintosh parcels, with just our faces showing, we stepped out into what was undeniably a flood.

"Hold tight," I told Sandy, as the water rushed up our calves.

Sloshing through the grubby tide, dead hedgehogs and fig boughs and a drowned kitten banged against our legs. The neighbour's house was full of buckets and dustbins catching leaks, sodden towels lay over the floor and bedraggled dogs and children shivered in front of the gas stove. Their wiring was so suspect they had switched everything off and the room smelt of vanilla candles. If the baker's was open we would bring back something for them.

Guttering spewed water like a fireman's hose, and we saw the woodcutter – his house for sale – with the door wide open, mopping brown sludge down the steps. It came down to which side of the sloping road you lived; you were damp or deluged. The baker had no power to bake bread and yesterday's leftovers were sold out. Catastrophe.

We were hailed by the Lady With Bunions.

"Monsieur, please, if you have time – can you help me? It is my piano and my carpet – they are so heavy I can't move them. If the water comes under the door..."

We went through her kitchen with its blazing fire, and into a parlour with an upright piano and a beautiful Oriental carpet.

"The rug was my father's," she said, wringing her hands, "and my husband loved this piano."

"They should be safe upstairs," I said, looking around for the staircase, and hoping it was a strong one.

She showed us a flight of wide stone steps behind a beaded curtain; a landing five steps up. We rolled the carpet and buckled under the weight of silk and wool; half-dragged, half-carried we got it up to the first floor. The piano had casters, which helped and hindered. It groaned and tinkled as we hefted it up to the landing.

"Stop! That will do!" said the Lady With Bunions. "It will be safe there."

"Are you sure, Madame?" I asked. "It hasn't stopped raining. The water is still rising."

"I've lived here for fifty years and I've seen lots of rain like this. My sons moved the piano this far many times. It will be fine there. Thank you, thank you very much."

"If you're sure...."

She became wistful.

"Nobody plays the piano any more," she said. 'When I was a child we all had lessons and my husband – he had golden fingers! He loved the hymns and he knew all the old songs. A bit of jazz too."

She lifted the lid and rippled off a few arpeggios.

"Let me see, what do I remember? How about this..?" she said with a sly smile.

We were treated to a fair rendition of 'Singing in the Rain', as we stood warming our hands by the fire. Saying we'd come and put everything back when the danger was over, we left to check on Madame Bernard a few houses along, but on the best side of the road.

"*Oui, c'est bon,*" she said. 'What about you in the old house? Are you dry? Are you warm? Are you hungry?"

There was a pot bubbling on the stove, and she had us strip off and sit by the fire while she ladled her soup into bowls and covered them with cheese.

"I'm sorry there's no bread," she shrugged.

Our mouths were too full to say it didn't matter.

Over three days the floods devastated the Gard, most roads unpassable, bridges swept away. More than thirty people dead or missing. Vineyards ruined. Oaks around since the Revolution torn up and turned to firewood. Landscapes became waterscapes, ducks swimming in and out of upstairs windows, cars in trees – a variation on Billie Holiday's 'Strange Fruit'. My favourite swimming hole was a small sea, littered with fossilised wood and mat-

MADAME BERNARD'S SOUP

tresses. Cement telegraph poles lay about like lead soldiers. A Roman viaduct, the Pont du Gard, survived intact, while modern buildings crumbled and collapsed. There was no drinking water in town and cafés and restaurants stayed closed. Owners of enviable riverside homes denied the right to rebuild; the risk too great. Everyone looked beaten and worried; their world had come to an end. We all felt small and vulnerable to the elements.

Being quite high and built on a gentle slope, our village came out of it well. The streets were ankle deep in foul water and then mud. We lost a few feral cats. Some houses had natural springs bubbling up through the floors, lifting ancient tiles and ruining plaster. Most, like ours, had been built with their backs to the weather, doors and windows on the leeward side, and the storm only tested their roofs. The main trunk road passing our lane was a torrent of water. We made coffee for the frightened drivers who pulled off it and parked outside, waiting for the respite that was a long time coming.

This is an area of 'big weather' and we will have to get used to it. Alex told us we'd survived our first 'Cevenol Event'; that they happened every decade or so. Biblical event more like. Now that we have Madame Bernard's recipe for soup, we'll be better prepared.

This is how the soup is made, as she told it to me.

"Cut up all the vegetables first, and make them all the same size. two cabbage leaves, one courgette – not too big, two potatoes, not too big – one leek, one stick of celery and some leaves, a handful of French beans, and the same of haricots, a couple of tomatoes and an onion.

"Use olive oil to fry the onion, not much, one or two spoons. Don't let them go brown, just a bit of colour. Put in the tomatoes next. When they are soft, pour in some stock, about a litre and wait until it boils. Put in all the other vegetables. After 10 or 12 minutes add some broken spaghetti, or you can buy a packet of little soup spaghetti. Leave it bubbling, not too strongly.

"Do you have a mortar and pestle? *Bon*, mix up in a mortar some garlic, four cloves is enough, and some fresh basil, about a dozen sprigs, until it is paste, and dribble in some olive oil. No more than three spoonfuls. It should be like cream to pour. I think you can buy this in jars now, if you don't have time to do it my way. I have lots of time.

"When the soup is ready, the potatoes will be soft. You take the pot away from the flame and put in the paste. Stir it gently.

"Put some Gruyère, grated on the smallest holes, into the bowls and pour the soup over.

"*Eh, voilà.*"

If you like, it is nothing more or less than a minestrone. She is right; her paste is pesto without the pine nuts, and pesto from a jar would be a good substitute. Not everyone has a mortar and pestle. Her haricot beans were dried, and she cooked them separately beforehand. You could use a tin; we do. This soup is a good way to use up broken pasta, but you can buy pastina, if you're not a frugal French housewife. *Eh, voilà.*

OF RATS AND MEN

THE RAIN STOPPED and the sun came out. Our close-up world was sodden, the countryside steamed like a laundry and all over central southern France there were puddles the size of Sussex.

We had three visitors. The first two we were expecting – Keith and Lesley, who came with cagoules and cardigans as well as shorts and sun-hats. Ex-Baloo and Brown Owl, prepared for most eventualities. They were curious about the house, looking forward to good food and wine and willing to muck in with the work.

Keith wanted to take a look at the local hunting scene; his imagination fired by the idea of winter weekends going after wild boar. Up before dawn on frosty mornings and out in the *garrigue*, as an antidote to stressful city life. As a cheese-aholic he was also on a pilgrimage and we had made a local list for him to try. It was the cheese version of the Beaufort scale of wind, from hurricane down to zephyr; from vintage Cantal to fresh *chevre* from the ostrich farm. There was even a real Beaufort cheese, if we could find it in the market; which was definitely a 'storm force 10'.

Lesley was going to soak up the atmosphere, swing in the hammock and spend spend spend at Uzès market, and both had a hankering to sing *'Sur le Pont d'Avignon'* at the tops of their voices, standing on the unfinished bridge. We were going to mix pain and pleasure, breaking bread at a picnic as well as breaking backs on the grindstone. Maybe some river swimming and wine tasting, along with the tree-lopping and stable clearing. Weather permitting.

And then the rat arrived.

We guessed he was another country gentleman, who had been flooded out like everyone else. Just after we'd moved in we'd caught glimpses of a 'big mouse' on early morning visits to the courtyard loo. There had been rodent skeletons in the stables and cartons of poisoned grain – dyed pink in case in a forgetful moment you might feed it to the chickens by mistake. So it wasn't the first time the old house had been a refuge. Living in the country meant adjusting to a certain amount of wildlife in your bed and your boots. Spiders as big and as black as bibles, a soft green praying mantis swaying to some inner song, hornets with the hump, swooping swallows and shy black scorpions. But a rat, you might say, was a horse of an entirely different complexion... .He was active at night, and Sandy, as a light sleeper, was woken by his hourly runs. We found droppings in our makeshift kitchen. He wasn't winning himself many friends.

Over the first few days of their holiday, as the rat became ever bolder, Keith and Lesley met him too. They told us about a mouse infestation in their first house, nightly scrabblings above the suspended ceiling, scattered cornflakes in the pantry. Traps didn't work, so they used poison and then had to dispose of dozens of tiny corpses. Were we sure it was only one rat?

We could cope with one, but not a whole family. With heavy hearts we decided he had to go. In the absence of any rat-charmers or pied pipers, on our next shopping trip we bought a trap and some chocolate, which Keith believed they preferred to cheese. Or perhaps he just couldn't bear the thought of a rat tucking into a good *brebis* or ripe *tomme*. We set the trap and put it along his usual run. Sandy heard him all night, but next morning the chocolate was gone and the trap unsprung. Sneaky rat.

Keith had another idea. Living in the country, he said, an air rifle would come in useful. For nabbing rabbits and wood pigeons for pies and *pâté*. He could go out with it too when he came for weekends. It would be a good investment – and we could use it to kill the rat. As a crack-shot with clays – annual winner of a Christmas turkey at the 'turkey shoot' – we had every confidence in him and set off to the local gun shop.

En route we speculated about the rules and regulations of owning a gun in France; attending an interview and registering with the gendarmes, finding somewhere to keep it under lock and key. A lot of time and trouble for a rat.

The gun shop was an Aladdin's cave for Keith. Ahead of the boar and deer hunting season, twelve bore shotguns lay about on the counter, awaiting servicing or collection. There were cartridges and bullets, hand-guns and rifles, none of them locked away; no CCTV or security doors. Keith was horrified and excited in equal measure. I was plain horrified having seen the price of the air rifles. 600 euros to dispatch one rodent – or even twenty – was extravagant. Not wanting to dampen Keith's enthusiasm, I asked the shopkeeper if he could suggest an alternative. At half the price of the air rifles, the.22s seemed like a good idea. Keith tried the gun for weight and balance, played with the mechanism. We chose a case and strap, oil and bullets and before you could say Jesse James we were ready to make mincemeat of the uninvited guest. The gunsmith explained the rifle was illegal for hunting, but... .he shrugged and held his hands like blinkers over his eyes. We thought it best not to mention our target.

Armed to the teeth we headed to the supermarket for more mundane shopping. We drank two cans of Coke and on our way home stopped off in the *garrigue* for some target practice. Setting the empty cans on a fallen oak we took turns to shoot, like the Jackal practising on melons before trying to assassinate de Gaulle. I heard no tell-tale pinging and thought we had missed. No power, I suggested. High velocity explained Keith; the bullets had gone straight through. Going back to the car Keith cut some forked branches of various lengths, on which to rest the gun for better aim on a moving target. 'Sayonara ratty'.

At the house Sandy and Lesley told us that the rat had brazenly stared at them in the garage for the last hour, retreating only at the sound of the car doors slamming. They pointed out a hole in the stones just where the vaulted ceiling joined the end wall.

"Right!" said Keith and set himself up with the gun and his aiming sticks.

Sitting in a director's chair, with a bottle of beer and cigarettes to hand, the Great White Hunter fixed his eye on the animal's lair and waited for his quarry. And waited. And waited. He kept up the vigil, happy as Hemingway hunting rhino, but the rat didn't show.

Outside the three of us made ourselves busy, waiting for the single shot.

EN GARD

Sandy and Lesley were knee-deep in old straw and sheep-shit. Using tin-snips they cut their way through several furlongs of rusty old wire. This lethal bird's nest of knots and barbs, tetanus lurking in every strand, had once held the previous owner's life together. In a few hours they had dismantled old chicken wire fences and untangled the cast-iron sheep-pens, bagging up the evil straw-muck as they went along. I fired up the new incinerator and stoked it with elder branches. Keith had hacked them down the day before, with 'Mr Grimsdale', as he christened the six year-old from next door. The kids were always trying to get involved, from washing-up to watering plants, and Keith, old Scout, had helped 'Mr Grimsdale' get his tree-craft badge....

Mino was attracted by the billowing white clouds produced by the wet wood and leaves.

"Sorry Mino," I said. "Is this smoke too much? Is It a problem?"

"Smoke never bothers gypsies," he grinned, "but a pastis would be good...

For the throat...." He coughed dramatically.

We went into the garage for the pastis and the iced water.

"Don't disturb Keith," I told him. "He's hunting rats!"

Mino's eyes are sharp and there are times when his mind is keen. A chance to turn a fast buck, an opportunity to look good at someone's expense, some physical danger. In the face of swindled clients or rent collectors he is like a mental cobra. And he was quick that evening too.

'"Stop! Put the rifle down – now!" In a flash he had seen the rifle, the bullets, the angle of elevation, the granite walls, the nature of ricochet, a tragedy in the making. Puzzled, Keith put the rifle down and Mino grabbed the box of bullets.

"Look at this –" he said pointing to the small print. I read the warning that the bullets could travel for two kilometres. Whether or not he hit the rat between the eyes, and he probably would have, the bullet could have continued, bouncing off the walls up to a distance of two kilometres – with Keith trapped in the middle. His own private Alamo. A little enthusiasm is a dangerous thing.

That night we went out to eat at a restaurant specialising in simple local dishes and famous for their cheeseboard. It declares

OF RATS AND MEN

proudly *'ici on mange gras'*, 'here we eat fat'. We ate huge *cepes* omelettes and got pleasantly sozzled. We were waiting for the cheese – especially the one which was *'anti-moustique'*, for keeping away mosquitoes – when a young couple, obviously hopelessly in love, asked Keith to take their candle-lit photograph. It started a chain of kissing photos including us, the lesbian waitress and the lone male diner, men and women from tables either side of the aisle. The sweetest orgy ever. A crazy Englishman gave them all a night to remember, on a day when he was lucky to be alive.

Keith and Lesley went home, but the rat stayed. By now Sandy's sleep was so interrupted she was hallucinating. Chariots and steam engines and hairy feet.

Enough. Enough. We bought some modern poison, laced chocolates with it and set the trap.

A few days later, while Sandy was making tea for a visitor, the rat fell from his hole in the wall and onto the plate of butter biscuits and banana cake Sandy had just prepared. The visitor, an animal lover and fierce anti-vivisectionist, screamed.

Sandy isn't a screamer, but she jumped back and swore like a sergeant major. The rat was trembling and looked comatose. Something quick and painless to finish it off was the humane thing to do.

'Alistair – DO something please!' said the visitor.

The incinerator was alight in the courtyard and I thought that would be the answer. I grabbed an old shoebox and approached the rat with a dustpan and broom, putting thoughts of Black Death, Weil's disease and throat biting cornered animals, right out of my mind. It might have been half-dead but the rat saw me coming. It reacted by leaping four feet into the air, crashing down again into the afternoon tea. My heart nearly burst out of my chest.

The visitor left, pale and shaken, and we scooped the rat and a lot of banana cake into the box and gave it a decent cremation among the elder embers.

November 22nd, 2002
Road Rage

Dear Den,
This is the letter that nearly never was. Coming back from town today we were nearly wiped out, not once, but twice.

I'm beginning to believe that's how I'm going to die – in a head-on crash with a pie-eyed Frenchman, with a poodle in his lap, driving some rusty old cake tin held together with string and bale-twine. Or by a boy-racer, fried on alcopops, deafened by rap, driving something low down and white, that sounds like a wardrobe being dragged over blunt rocks.

I haven't said as much to Scotty. One of my two superstitions is that saying something can often make it happen – the other is that unless I use the same coloured pegs on separate bits of clothing on the washing line, harm will come to those I love; so far so good.

Sorry, the French are wonderful people, I could hug them all, but they drive like bastards.

The road that comes this way out of Uzès isn't wide, it was built for horse-drawn traffic. Two carts could pass easily and, if it wasn't busy, stop for a chat about the price of eggs. If it was busy, all three drivers could stop, and really put the world to rights.

The first few kilometres of the road are lined with plane trees. Napoleon ordered them to be planted all over France, so that his troops could always march in shade. Now it's the army of tourists driving into market all summer who benefit from the shade. Big and beautiful as the trees are, and part of France's history, it's hard to think about cutting them down, just to widen the road. And so we have wacky races.

There is a monstrous movement which believes that the trees are responsible for hundreds of deaths a year. It's campaigning for them all to be chopped down. As most of those deaths are young men, full of alcohol, losing control of fast cars, it seems a bit rough to blame the old trees. Hard for a parent to blame their dead child; to admit his culpability. Much, much easier to trash the trees. True, if they weren't there, no-one

ROAD RAGE

could hit them. They would hit walls or end up in ditches. The c**ts would hit something.

Along the avenue, posies of silk or plastic flowers are nailed to the treetrunks. A reminder, for anyone going slow enough to see them, that humans, with our thin skulls and thick heads, usually come off worst. The pathetic flowers are preferable to the gruesome silhouettes with red hearts that mark motoring black spots. I counted seven in a group once, standing close to the barrier – like Zorro without his hat. In the early days we wondered what they were advertising. Death, as it turns out.

For our information, the government displays the annual death toll on a bad stretch of road. Those figures climb, year on year. Drivers must see them more as targets to be met and exceeded, than sorry testimony to their impatience and addiction to booze and fifth gear.

When you consider the French man or woman in any other aspect of their daily lives – amiable, courteous, caring – the French motorist is an aberration.

And here's a dangerous threesome – a Frenchman, a car and a phone. Common or garden mobiles mean one hand for the phone and one for waving to emphasise the point he's making; hands-free sets mean he can wave both hands; texting, he can keep one hand on the wheel, but can't watch the road. My heart sinks when I see a learner accelerating towards a pedestrian crossing; please, no more.

Our narrow squeaks happened on the hill climb. This is a series of chicanes, with a drop off to the right, maybe a hundred feet, into the garrigue. Lots of gaps in the wall, where someone misjudged it in the dark, or after a good lunch. An eldest son was killed by his neighbour's van here. Ugly graffiti in red dripping letters appeared on the wall. "Tu payeras!" – "You will pay!" Drivers coming down the hill like to keep to the racing-line, which has nothing at all to do with the white line in the middle of the road. They maintain the racing-line at a racing speed, around blind corners, talking to their mistresses on a mobile. Or in lorries full of lumber, shrouded in dust, windscreen obscured by cuddly toys, feeding sausage to a dog on the passenger seat.

Today, we were lucky, but it is only a matter of time.

Notwithstanding all this, I'm supposed to be learning to drive. Otherwise, in a village with one bus a day I rely entirely on other people – usually Scotty, who has plenty of other things to do. Putting me in a car into this equation might be the catalyst that hastens my sticky end.

I've been on my high-horse a bit, and I didn't intend to spend most of a letter raging. Not much space left to thank you for your recipes, and to be amazed that you might soon be back on a film set.

I'm going to try the carrot cake first, as it's foolproof, because every other one I've tried ended up like a geological specimen, and in the bin.

You're going to love being back in the 'industry', even if it is backstage. A chance to put feelers out. Legs crossed that it all goes ahead. Look forward to seeing your name on the credits between 'best boy' and 'head gaffer'.

The next letter will be chilled and less full of itself.

Best love, Sandy and Scotty.

DEUX PETITS CANARDS – 22

THE LAST VILLAGE party had been in October and, as the nights grew longer, shutters closed earlier, keeping the warmth in and the casual visitor out.

During the day the streets were empty, though you might glimpse Madame Bernard in woolly hat and quilted dressing-gown on the way to her woodpile. Nothing much was moving. Besides games of snakes and ladders with the kids next door, pastis with their parents and tapas with the district nurse, we'd been moribund and catching up on sleep.

In the second week of February there were signs to suggest that Spring was not too far away; wild violets in the courtyard and almond trees in full bloom and the occasional days of hot sunshine to counter the sub-zero nights.

One of the sunny days we spent woodcutting and stacking. It's hard, dirty and satisfying work. At the end of it you have splinters, bruised fingers, a bad back and a beautiful pyramid of oak logs.

We were pleasantly tired and monosyllabic when Lola arrived to share some good news. The hospital had given her the all-clear on a long-standing problem, and she wanted to celebrate.

"We should have a night out," she announced, and at that moment her husband turned up.

"We've decided to celebrate with a night on the town tomorrow," she told him. I wasn't aware we'd decided any such thing.

" ...at Bingo," Lola finished excitedly.

Too tired to think on our feet, to invent another commitment, to plead an attack of shingles or plague, we'd been out-manoeuvred. Rico slumped. I slumped. Sandy managed a weak smile. If I were to draw up a list of ten things I least wanted from a night out, Bingo would come just above branding with hot irons. It was no better for Sandy, who thought sleeping with spiders a pretty good alternative.

EN GARD

Lola talked enthusiastically and optimistically about the outing, and the rest of us downed some pastis and cringed.

"Bingo," I said when they had gone. "I'll never live this down. Imagine what it's going to be like – some smarmy lounge lizard, all slicked-back Brylcream and pencil moustache. He'll probably have a sequinned jacket. Firing foreign numbers at us for hours on end. What about all the patter that goes with it? *Deux petits canards – 22; deux grosses dames – 88; jambes – 11; douce 16 – jamais* been kissed or something. I'll go effing mad!"

"Just this once," said Sandy to comfort us both. "And never, ever again. It'll make Lola happy."

"No-one must ever know." I said. "We'd be ruined."

The next evening Lola knocked on the door a full 15 minutes early. That was a measure of her excitement. We headed off in Rico's car and he looked like he was on his way to the guillotine. Lola pointed out a broken down old building.

"That's where Bingo used to be held, but they've moved to a bigger place now."

My heart sank a little more.

Two roundabouts later and Rico turned the car into an industrial zone.

"That's the place," said Lola, her door open before Rico had the handbrake on. She half-guided and half-dragged Sandy across the car park to the entrance.

"Pah," said Rico, "we're far too early. Let's have a smoke."

By the time we followed them in, Lola had explained the finer points to Sandy. She recommended eight cards each. These could be bought on a plaque – a cardboard sheet – and cost twelve euros. You could win with one line, two lines or a full house.

"Please win," I said to Sandy. 'I want to hear you shout '*Maison*'!'"

There was no lounge lizard, just a team of scruffy men, Gaulloise welded in the corners of their mouths, in a corrugated iron industrial unit. Huge extractor fans to cope with a thousand cigarettes, sucked hard in concentration to red hot tips. Early in the evening there was already a thick pall of smoke, like something from Bhopal. Long rows of plastic tables and chairs with waiters swooping between them and a cross-section of the population seated at them. Grandmothers and grandchildren, courting couples, divorcing couples, lonely middle-aged men and, as you would expect, raucous packs of female friends. Only teenage boys were conspicuously absent, somehow finding cold street corners and a shared bottle of Fanta more attractive.

"I need a drink," I said to Rico.

"Oh, *non*," he said, "there's no alcohol."

Two of the scruffy men were the 'callers'. Using a public address system bought second-hand from a local scout group, they called us to order. Neither Sandy nor I could understand a distorted word they said, and this did not bode well for an evening of strange numbers.

Sandy can't really cope with the French number system after 70. She's bewildered by the idea of 4x20+8 being 88, or 4x20+17, spoken as four, twenty, ten, seven, being 97. It was going to be necessary to concentrate very hard indeed.

We were lucky to have Lola. When Rico dozed off she took up the role of bingo-caller-stars-in-her-eyes. She did everything – she repeated the numbers, she scanned her own eight cards, then Sandy's and then mine. She stabbed at the numbers on our cards when we had to place a counter on one of our squares. It was awful for me. Sandy glazed over.

With Lola in complete control, I had time to look around. The man next to me had thirty-six cards on the go. His eyes moved faster than balls in a pinball machine. His hand was a blur distributing counters around his plaque. He had missed a vocation as a ping-pong professional, or an air traffic controller.

I pleaded fatigue and the need for fresh air, and squeezed past a dozing Rico. I watched a woman who was manic. She had 48 cards. Everytime someone else in the room called out with winning lines, or a full house, she cried out as if she had been impaled.

Sandy nearly won twice, each time waiting for the number 5. Lola pointed it out to those around her as if there was an awful conspiracy at work.

"New players always win on their first visit," they agreed.

Midnight came and went and I wished I could join Rico in

EN GARD

sleepy oblivion but Lola's excitement was too much. I told Sandy I was worried about deep vein thrombosis, and I needed a walk. I only got as far as a grandmother. She had her hand inside the right cup of her bra and she forcefully squeezed her breast everytime a number was called. Like Italian and Arab men grabbing their genitals to ward off the evil eye. She still needed four numbers for a full house. She squeezed harder. I did not want to be there if she required only one number.

I went back to the table when my blood circulation was normal. There was a lull in the proceedings and a chance to relax.

"Lola," I asked, "what do we stand to win?"

"Hundreds of euros," she said.

"What – cash?"

"*Non*," she explained, "The *gendarmes* stopped that. It's shopping vouchers for Monoprix." I knew Monoprix. It is the French Woolworths.

"Superb!" I said to Lola, so as not to burst her bubble. I worked it out quickly – two full houses and I could have five hundred 1970s Sacha Distel cassettes. I was rapidly losing the will to live.

"What time does it finish?" I asked.

"Not yet," said Lola, "there are a few more games to go."

But I was fading fast. I handed my card to Lola, who now had everyone's card except Sandy's, and lay my head on the table beside Rico.

None of us won a thing. Sandy is still waiting for number 5. There were no '*deux petits canards*' – 22. Instead 22 is ' *les gendarmes*'; 44 - 'two little chairs'; 'the peanut' – 8; and French department numbers featured strongly. 'Aveyron' – 12, 'Corsica' – 20, '*Chez nous*' – 30, with 'our neighbours' 34. And no-one shouted '*Maison!*'. Just '*Allez-oop!*' very loudly.

As we said goodnight, Lola made a point of telling us that there were many more games on Saturdays and Sundays if we were interested.

"Never, ever again," said Sandy as we climbed into bed.

"'Never is a long time in Bingo,'" I thought, but did not say it.

April 8th, 2003
Wild food & April fish

Sue,
I was settling down to start this letter two hours ago, when our neighbour arrived with a fistful of wild asparagus. She had spent the morning at one of her secret countryside larders, where she goes fruiting and mushrooming and where she finds her Christmas holly with big fat berries. Alistair and I are her good friends; but not so good that she will share her secret places with us. Another ten years maybe.

Wild asparagus is about as thick as a pencil and spindly; woody, apart from the end and the next inch. Thinking of a plate of my grandfather's garden asparagus, great green torpedoes, it made me realise that genetic engineering has been around a long time.

She's given us enough for a soufflé omelette and made me repeat back to her, word for word, the instructions for making it – as if I was going to remove an appendix blindfolded. Then I made the mistake of asking if wild asparagus grows around here. And off we went to look. The ramble took us down a track towards a cherry orchard. It's land the family want to buy, in case it becomes 'constructible' in a few years. She told me to come and help myself to cherries in June – the owner is housebound and always lets them rot. It's a peaceful spot, with a pretty view of the village. A good place to build a house if it were possible. No asparagus. On a bit further to their old stables and a good look round for anything to sell at the 'vide grenier', the village car boot sale. I came away with an ancient wooden pyramid ladder, used for picking fruit trees – just a little bit of worm in one leg. A death trap, but good to grow jasmine through. No asparagus.

By the time we got back, her kids were home from school, and in our courtyard to water the plants. This takes a bit of supervision – to avoid drenching or drowning or infanticide.

So, two hours later, when my sunny spot is in shade and my forgotten cup of tea is stone cold, I'm sitting down to write.

EN GARD

Whole days would evaporate like that, if you let them. Being your own master carries heavy responsibilities, which puts some salt on the freedom. You need self-discipline, but you have to gently educate everyone else, that being at home, for us, is being at work. No doubt that our lives are better. Harder physically and not much money to throw about, but the sense of well-being is wonderful. I remember listening to a cynic on late night radio saying ''Welcome to London – where to smile is a sign of weakness.'' and he went on to describe the English as ''a cold people in a cold climate''. Here, to smile is to have it returned; no strings. And it's hard to be cold in the face of relentless hospitality, courtesy and 'joie de vivre'.

It isn't perfect and neither are we. Chat and chien arguments are not unknown, but they are fewer and with less heat in them. They peter out, if we get distracted by beetles or birds or buds on the roses. At this time of the year the courtyard is full of red and black insects called 'gendarmes' – because they go around in pairs and are everywhere. We're still not agreed whether the pattern on their backs is a Zulu shield or Groucho Marx's face...

We still have a lot to learn. I went into the posh chocolate shop in Uzès last week. It was full of chocolate fish in foil, head to tail in tins, like sardines. The woman explained that it was 'Poisson d'Avril', a tradition. I forgot all about it. The next day, Djojo told us, very solemnly, that his father had fallen off scaffolding, and was in hospital. We rushed next door, wondering when his family's bad luck was ever going to end. Lola looked at us blankly when we asked how Rico was, and Djojo shouted 'Poisson d'Avril!'; April Fish/Fool, and gave us a chocolate sardine. Next year we'll be ready.

I'm enclosing some flyers and publicity. These are some of the things we might do, after a hard day's work – if we could stay awake long enough; if we could scrub up clean enough. As well as organised theatre and exhibitions, there are dozens of ad hoc performances, in front of busy cafes in the summer. A couple of people, with a suitcase of props give an hour of play or mime. Usually serious and way over my head. Quintessentially French.

Hope the Easter egg hunt goes well – chocolate or painted? We've been asked not to cut the grass in our garden, so that Lola can hide the kids' eggs there on Sunday. When she was a child, the real eggs they found

WILD FOOD AND APRIL FISH

were made into a giant family omelette on Easter Monday – but nowadays they are just chocolate ones, 'three for two' in the supermarket.

Wishing you a safe and happy trip to the States and hoping you find your mother in good spirits,

Best love,

Sandy and Alistair.

PAELLA PARTY

Ingredients
A sack of rice
The wings and legs of 16 chickens
A bucket of mussels
34 GIANT prawns
A few bags of smaller prawns
A string of mild onions
Red and green peppers, 5 of each
Saffron, as much as you can afford
A drunken 'pinch' of salt
A packet of frozen peas

34 people looking for a good time
My brother and his wife
A young tenor
A philosophical child
An acrobatic sister-in-law
A loaded shotgun
A violent temper
Pastis
Whisky

AS LIFELONG disciples of one-pot cooking, paella is a dish made in Heaven for Sandy and me. Strong flavours, pick and mix ingredients and not much washing-up. We cook enough to last two days, except for the mussels – which we eat in one go, just to be safe. There was a pan of paella sitting on the stove one day, when Lola came by to 'borrow' some eggs.

"What's this? – aahh paella!" she said, picking up a fork and flicking it over; helping herself to some juicy titbits.

"It's not a proper one," she said through a mouthful of prawns. "It's not a gypsy paella, cooked on a wood fire, in a pan as big as this –" she held her arms out to her sides, "with music and dancing...we should have a party, and I'll show you what paella really is!"

Sandy and I thought a paella party would be an amazing start to my brother's holiday. If we could have the party when Ian and Ann arrived, it would give them a flavour of Gardoise gypsy hospitality, something they would never forget. If Lola was serious.

Lola was happy to do it. Why miss an opportunity to get dolled-up, boss your husband about, get drunk and dance yourself

PAELLA PARTY

dizzy? Lola had been born out of her time really. She was a gypsy wife and mother, instead of a lap-dancer or an actress or a politician. Although, at family festivities she sometimes managed to combine all these roles.

"We'll do the shopping on Thursday," she said, and we agreed to meet at the supermarket.

"One trolley should be enough," Lola said, grabbing one and heading into the shop.

Sandy and I exchanged a look. Why wouldn't one trolley be enough for a family party?

We went first to the fruit and vegetable section, where Lola crammed cherries into her mouth, keeping an eye out for security. She put a whole string of onions and a large mixed bag of peppers in the cart.

"I've got plenty of onions and peppers at home," said Sandy. Lola ignored her.

The vegetables were quickly followed by a sack of rice and a sachet of saffron, costing the earth – and the moon and the stars.

"Lola, stop," Sandy was perplexed. "Why do we need so much of everything? There's enough for an army here!"

"Didn't I tell you?" Lola looked sheepish. "Hervé's wife heard we were doing a paella, so I had to invite her, and Hervé too of course; Hervé drinks with Djimmy and so I had to ask Djimmy, and that means Cécile too. Cécile's friend is staying for the weekend, with her boyfriend, so it would be rude not to invite them. He is a beautiful singer, and he usually sings with his sister and so..."

She went on like this until 34 people, most of whom we had never met, were coming to our 'cosy' family party. It was like Genesis; one invitation had begat another, begat another. We thought of Ian and Ann, and how they would enjoy it. Something they would never forget. We'd go along with it.

Trays of chicken thighs were piled in the trolley and Lola tossed bag after bag of frozen prawns on top of them. She stopped at seven, and then, on reflection, added an eighth. A bag of frozen peas as big as a pillow. And then at the fresh fish counter the mussels didn't meet with her approval. Lola took a handful and pressed them to her nose. She dropped them like hot coals, wrinkled her face and shivered,

"Disgusting! They must be days old," she said loudly.

So we had to buy Dutch mussels, alive and vacuum-packed in sea water, at three times the price. She chose 34 giant prawns, picking over the pile, prawn by prawn, discarding the undersized or broken, until she was satisfied. The woman serving at the counter gave her a look to kill; grist to the mill for Lola.

A jerrycan of olive oil, and wine and whisky for the five thousand. One trolley was only just enough. We headed for the checkout, and on the way Lola threw in one more bag of prawns. For luck... Or greed.

"Oh my God..." said Sandy, and she clutched my arm.

"What? What's wrong?" I thought she was having a heart-attack.

"Look!" she said, pointing at Lola. "She hasn't brought her handbag!"

"We're paying for all of this? Have we got the money?"

It wasn't our habit to walk around with pockets full of cash, and we'd come shopping for a 'family party' not for a full-blown fiesta. The shopping cleaned us out. We had one euro and twenty-six cents left. Lola didn't say a word or offer a sou. Imagining, I think, that her contribution was 'Theatre de Lola', the cooking, the dancing, the drama of the evening, and that, plus the salt and pepper, was enough.

My brother and his wife arrived on a late flight and the party was set for the next night.

"It'll be an experience," we said "something to remember."

The party was going to be Lola's show, but she needed a few handmaidens for the dirty work. Someone to cry peeling the onions, to break fingernails scrubbing the mussels. Sandy and Ann got the job. The following afternoon was spent chopping, slicing, cleaning and washing all the ingredients, under Lola's critical eye and sharp tongue.

Her husband, Rico, and a couple of sons, were dragged away from a drunken game of *boules*, to build the fire and to find the paella pan, the size of a cartwheel, buried under piles of junk in their garage. Rico got his orders to make something for stirring the

PAELLA PARTY

paella; something wide and flat, with a long handle which wouldn't get hot. The great pan was found; blackened and scarred and needing a good wash... Like a cast-iron temple-gong, best played with the thigh bone of an Englishman. I hoped we had enough food to fill it.

In the early evening, the bats came out to play and the tree frogs honked lonely unrequited love. Party guests arrived, some in time for the sunset; all in time for pastis and *kir*. The gypsy game we called 'trumping' began. My car is flashier and newer than yours, among the men; my jewellery is flashier and older than yours, amongst the women. Engines were revved and bonnets raised; earrings were swung and rings held up to catch the light. Pastis and whisky flowed freely, and hunger, like a small whiskery animal, began to gnaw at us.

Enter stage left, Lola. Hair in tangled curls, pinned in a knot by gold combs, eyes outlined in black, lids violet, lips red. Barefoot and wearing nothing very much under a skimpy white dress. A dozen gold hoops in each ear and a large pastis in her hand. Like a society hostess, she butterfly kissed and ruffled the hair of all her guests, making her way centre-stage to the empty pan sitting on the unlit fire. The husky voice called for action, and terrifyingly tattooed men scurried about like mice.

The fire was lit, and the gypsies moved closer to it, attracted like magnets or moths. Breeze blocks were placed on opposite ends of the fire to support the pan, and a pile of extra wood placed within easy reach. A table was set up, to take the dishes of prepared meat, fish and vegetables which were laid out in the order they would go into the pan. Add military general to the list of Lola's unfulfilled ambitions.

The flames died to embers and she called for more wood. Rico used all the branches from the pile and then attacked our priceless stack of dry oak. He fanned the flames with a dustbin lid and the kids helped, using tin plates and frying pans. Rico produced his 'stirrer', made from a broom handle with a spatula whipped to one end. Sandy told him he was very creative and he puffed up with pride.

Lola threw back her head, emptying her glass of pastis, stubbed out her cigarette against the wall, and moved into the firelight. The hubbub died down as Rico put the pan over the glowing logs.

"Bring me the olive oil and the chicken!" she commanded, and her sister-in-law obeyed.

Lola crouched low and poured the oil, spilling some into the fire for pyrotechnic effect. She added the chicken pieces, which hissed and spat as she turned them this way and that to brown, like an ice-hockey player with a puck.

"A bucket!" she shouted, and put the sizzling chicken in it.

"Peppers and onions, Sandy!" she called. "And pastis – can't a cook get a drink around here?" Lola handed the stirrer to Sandy, and told her to keep the vegetables moving so they wouldn't burn. The heat from the fire was enough to keep Sandy moving too, so she didn't burn. The nutty sweetness of cooked onions, the caramelisation, only happens over a high heat. We could smell this going on and combined with the luscious chicken in the bucket, our juices were running.

"Alistair – bring the hose!" Lola took over again "Rico – bring the rice!"

Water and rice went into the pan, and Lola emptied the chicken on top, stirring with two hands, legs braced, like a sorceress with attitude.

"Hose me down Alistair, my legs are cooking!" she cried.

I thought she was joking and laughed. She grabbed the hose from my hands and turned it on herself from the neck down. The white dress became transparent. She shook her hair loose and wet that too, flinging it back, and ran the water over her legs. She had a slug of pastis, and was back in action.

The bottom of the old pan was so pitted and damaged that there were hot and cold spots. The rice had to be kept moving or it wouldn't cook evenly. It was hot and thirsty work. I took over from Lola for a while. My legs were cooking too, and the third son turned the hose on me. Full on. Crazy little bastard. Luckily sawn-off Levis don't become transparent.

My brother and his wife were capturing it all on film from the safety of the terrace steps. The camera saved them from the drenching that Lola was plotting, and she went off in search of

PAELLA PARTY

other victims among her sons' friends.

The cooking gathered momentum. Saffron went into the rice, and then in rapid succession, the mussels and prawns and frozen peas. Trestle tables were put together by confused drunken men, the cloths and cutlery laid by slightly merry wives. The tables were only at a slight angle, and everyone got at least one fork. Seats were improvised from planks, upturned bins and boxes and the kids sat cross-legged on some straw on the ground. The paella pan was too big and heavy to be moved, so we queued to be served, like orphans from 'Les Miserables'.

"What d'you think?" I asked Ian and Ann, meaning the food and the 'Theatre de Lola'.

"Bloody good," said Ian, meaning both.

Plates were piled high and no-one went back for seconds. The floor was cleared, the music pumped up and the dancing began. 'Gypsy Kings' and less hyped, rougher gypsy bands stirred the blood; women danced alone and with other women, in a mild trance. Fingers clicked, feet stamped, hair tossed, sweat broke out on upper lips. The men were aloof, watching with half an eye that their wives were behaving themselves, but more intent on 'trumping' with their friends.

Lola put up with this for a while. Then she wanted some attention. The music changed to something pulsing and carnal. Lap-dancing without the laps. She ran her hands over her body, caressing her breasts, swayed her hips, thrust her pelvis up against Rico, who carried on his conversation. She threw herself past him, to use the door as a prop. She made love to it; licking and stroking the door-knob, her hands clutched the curtains like a lover's clothes, she moaned loudly in time with the music.

"Bloody hell!" said Ian.

Rico was deep into a discussion about rendering and oblivious to Lola. She stopped the exotic dance routine and marched over to him, hands on hips. She prodded him in the chest.

"Hey you! Who do think I'm dancing for? I'm doing all this for your benefit and you can't even be bothered to look! You don't deserve me – you'd be happy with some fat old trout with legs a pig could run through."

EN GARD

She tore him away from the group of rendering experts, and demanded some smoochy music. At this point, most of the young men drifted away from the party. They climbed into old bangers with go-fast stripes, gunned the engines and disappeared into the night in search of less embarrassing entertainment.

The cheek-to-cheek dance over, Lola went over to a young man sitting quietly in the corner. She took his hand and gently coaxed him into the middle of the room, telling someone to turn the music off and the rest of us to shut up and listen. A mellow tenor swelled *a cappella* in the shabby kitchen, and any residual chat soon stopped. Like lusty cream, the beautiful voice switched from Verdi to Cole Porter to Ray Charles and back to Verdi. His eyes fixed above our heads, somewhere between the cuckoo clock and some fly-paper, as he sang he changed the mood of the party – we turned from happy drunks to thoughtful ones. He stopped shyly, to applause and wolf whistles, and refusing the calls for an encore, went back to his seat with a beaming smile.

The women got up to dance again, and Lola brought out bits and pieces of flamenco costume, red frilly armbands and ruffled skirts. Sandy and Ann joined in, climbing into the skirts and practising a few bullfighter swirls and a bit of foot-stamping. Lola's sister-in-law, a woman in her forties with the face and body of a twelve-year-old, was getting frisky. A circus tumbler in her youth, she'd lost none of the suppleness or nerve, and with enough pastis inside her, she was wont to perform. Lola was her chosen partner, her straight man, to catch her as she flipped and did the splits. Running the length of the room to jump with scissored legs around Lola's waist, falling backwards to walk on her hands, tumbling or cart wheeling towards the china cabinet. Sandy and Ann kept practising their foot-stamping and their swirls.

The door into the kitchen burst open. Two of the young men who'd gone off in cars earlier, told Rico that his second son had got into a fight. The second son is the strong silent type, with a temper like cordite. Rico had to be held down by six of us, as he tried to get into his car, too drunk to focus. He wouldn't be calmed, until a friend of Lola's, cold sober, offered to drive him to the bar. The young men who had brought the news, told some of us that

PAELLA PARTY

the fight had been in full-swing when they left. They thought someone in the bar had slipped away to get a knife or a gun. When the eldest son heard this, he slipped away from our group. He reappeared with something wrapped in a blanket under his arm. His shotgun.

"Djimmy!" I said. "Don't be fucking stupid."

"My brother is in trouble, Alistair – I have to help him," he slurred.

"You're not getting past me with that thing. There are thirty people here watching you if you try and set off with a fucking shotgun. You can't help anybody with a gun."

But it wasn't me who stopped him. At that moment Lola came out onto the terrace. Djimmy knew that his mother would kill him herself, if she saw him with the gun. He darted back to the garage before she caught sight of it. The mood of the party had changed again, and this time I thought it was terminal. Sandy and Ann wandered over to the Temple steps, and sat down beside a little boy with his head in his hands.

"*Ça va?*" Sandy asked.

"Not really," he said. 'I've got a geometry test in the morning – I should be in bed by now."

"I think the party is nearly over," said Sandy. 'You can go home soon."

"How can I go home? My mother has driven away with Rico. I don't know when she's coming back."

Sandy put her arm round his shoulders, and said she was sorry that adults always seem to ruin things, especially if they drink alcohol. The little boy nodded and looked even sadder.

"Whisky destroys lives," he said and shook his head slowly.

I walked over to see how the girls were surviving the latest bombshell, and Sandy introduced me.

"I already know you," he said. "We played football. You taught me to kick with my left foot. I remembered what you told me. It helped me a lot."

"He's worried about his geometry test tomorrow," Sandy explained.

"Let's see if I can help you with that," I said to him.

EN GARD

I drew some triangles in the sand with a stick, and wrote in two angles, asking him to calculate the third. He knew all the answers and warmed to the task. Just as we were working out the height of a skyscraper, his mother came back with Rico.

The fight had been his son's fault, he discovered. As the son had disappeared at the mention of guns, Rico had apologised for him and promised that the boy would be back to apologise himself. He'd paid for the damage to the bar, and sobered up too much, and now he wanted to get on with the party.

But it was too late. There was no heart left in it. We could have carried on drinking and dancing, but we would have been faking it. It was over, and people were calling out their thanks and their goodbyes. The four of us sat for a while on the temple steps and doodled in the sand with sticks.

"I'm sorry it ended the way it did," I said.

"All part of the rich tapestry," said Ann. "You did say it would be a night to remember!"

FLUSHING OUT SOME LOCAL HISTORY

TWO THINGS FORCE us to start work. The first is necessity. If something is about to fall down, better to take it down and avoid the accident. If that something is a roof, you need to put up the replacement straightaway. A house without a roof isn't a house – it's just walls and soon becomes a ruin. To make our house a home, new roofs were a necessity and that's how they got done.

The second way we start work is through 'the cycle'. It begins with a week of nightmares about all the things that can go wrong. Followed by a week of sleeplessness, when, as the village clock chimes two and three, demons are whispering in your ear. The problem is insoluble, disaster inevitable. Nothing to fear but fear itself. It is the paralysing part of the cycle. We move on to displacement activities – weeding, laundry, chopping wood, cooking ever more complex meals, hours in the preparation. Anything to avoid the immense hard work, its dangers and, especially, our ignorance of the skills required. The penultimate part of the cycle is shame and guilt at our avoidance and inactivity, followed at last by a hankering to get on with it. In starting, the fear is replaced by an adrenaline rush at doing something new and strange, and a determination to do it as well as we can.

This is the way it was with the sewerage system.

We mentioned to the neighbours that we'd had enough of sitting on the Porta-potti under an umbrella, and that we were going to put in drains. They suggested that we talk to a 'local expert'. In the months to come, those were two words that would make our blood run cold many times. This local expert, a general builder with 60 years' experience, was expected at the neighbour's house for dinner this evening. Happy coincidence. I joined them for a pastis and to glean any information that might be forthcoming.

Monsieur Expert liked his pastis. This wasn't his first today. More like his twenty-first. He was listing badly in his chair. With

EN GARD

heavy eyelids and red rheumy eyes, he assured me, with the slightest of slurs, that he knew the area intimately. In particular, he knew for certain that there was no mains drainage for us to plumb into; not in this village. Every house must have its own septic tank. I didn't want to impugn his local expertise, but, before we bought the house, our estate agent had established otherwise. Later, at a village party, a lifelong resident had told me he remembered the drains going in. He'd worked for the Mairie at the time and recalled the cost and the problems. The young mayor had confirmed this too. "*Non, monsieur,*" the expert insisted, "there is no such system here."

"The mayor told me..." I began.

"*Non,* monsieur," he interrupted, affronted and waving his forefinger from side to side.

"*D'accord,*" I was polite, but sounded doubtful. He knew I didn't believe him.

"Come, I will show you." He lurched out of the chair and headed for the street, Rico and I following closely.

"That," he said pointing to a cast iron manhole cover, "is for your drinking water. That one over there is the phone company. Those," he swung round with a sweeping arm, "are the same, but for your neighbours. There is nothing, *monsieur*, absolutely nothing here like a cover for sewers. And I should know." he finished, tapping the side of his nose with a finger, the local sign for wisdom.

He thought I was a fool. I felt one. Perhaps I had misunderstood everything I'd been told by the others. After all, he was a local expert.

"Monsieur, there is one more cover at the bottom of the road. May we just take a look at it?" I asked.

"As you wish. BUT THERE ARE NO VILLAGE SEWERS!" At the sound of slightly raised voices, we had acquired a few hangers-on, keen to add their opinions too.

"*Oui,* monsieur, it is another cover. For what I do not know. I know what it is not. It is not for drains." The expert had an audience and he was enjoying it.

"Well, it must be for something," said Pedro, the last to join the group, now sixteen strong. "Let's take a look."

"Not sewers!" the expert was resolute.

I sent one of the kids off to fetch a crowbar from my garage. We took it in turns to lever the cover and three strapping lads lifted it off. Synchronised, all sixteen of us bent over the hole, keen to know who would put a hole, with a cover, in the road, for no purpose. As we stared down into the darkness, on cue, some clumps of yellow toilet tissue drifted by at the bottom of the hole.

"SEWERS!" went the chorus.

The expert straightened slowly in keeping with his years. Giving himself thinking time, he stroked his walrus moustache, pursed his lips, closed one eye slowly as his face twisted in anguish.

"That," he said facing the crowd, "that, should not be there."

He mustered some dignity, and turned back up the hill, to the comfort of his pastis glass. No one spoke; age is respected here even in a sozzled local expert.

Happy that we really did have a system to join on to, next we tried to agree on a layout for the finished house. In designing-in the bathrooms we had to take account of the bedrock. The house was built without foundations, directly on to vast slabs of granite. Depending on to whom you spoke this was somewhere between 100 and 1,000 metres deep. We could bring tubing out of the walls, but the large-bore pipes, taking away grey water and sewerage, would have to be buried in this granite as they crossed the courtyard. When our house and the neighbour's was all one, all 27 rooms of it, it was their half which was plumbed. There must have been a break, a path through the rock that way. So our side became the animal shelters because their toilet arrangements were much simpler.

We decided on two bathrooms, one above the other, next to the garage. This would give us the shortest run through the whaleback of granite, out into the road. Both rooms were large enough for a loo, shower and basin. On the ground floor there was space for a bath and the water heater. We might squeeze in a washing machine too. In a house without corridors, easy access to bathrooms was vital and these two rooms afforded that.

EN GARD

The next important preparation was to chart exactly where the granite ran; to see if there were any easy ways out. We doubted it. Opting for our usual stone-age tools, instead of expensive geophysics, we hammered iron rods through the topsoil every twelve inches. We found the two routes we wanted out to the road; one from the bathrooms and one from the kitchen on the opposite side of the courtyard. Granite extended three feet out from the bathroom wall, after which there was a long stretch of deep soil which ran the length of the garage. At the end of the garage to turn 90° towards the road we hit the first tranche of unavoidable rock. It was five feet long. The channel across this for the pipes needed to be 12 inches across and 18 inches deep. After this it was more deep soil out to the gates. So far, so good. The second line of pipes would come out of the house from the kitchen. This posed different problems. There was the concreted floor of the summer kitchen to go through, or under; then the root system of a large beautiful tree to be negotiated. Another 4ft of bedrock to cut through before freewheeling into rocky soil in the centre of the courtyard. A Y-bend here would join the two lines together, on out to the gates – and civilisation.

We were as ready as we were ever going to be to start. My brother and his wife arrived with perfect timing, fresh and enthusiastic.

'We'll hire a bloody great pneumatic drill and have it done in no time." What we found was a bloody great pneumatic jackhammer. The man in the hire shop would stake his life on its power and suitability for the job. Never having used a jackhammer before I wasn't clear about the technique. Did I put all my weight behind it? Did it do all the work? The noise shattered the peaceful village lunch hour; the machine shattered me. My teeth rattled, my joints jarred. Hundred of impacts every minute blurred the courtyard; everyone and everything in it out of focus. It was like riding a bucking bronco. I couldn't co-ordinate my bouncing with the hammer bouncing. Ann was leaning against a wall 12 feet away.

"I can feel the vibrations," she said, fragile old mortar dusting her shoulders.

I didn't stop. Thousands of short sharp shocks for me and the rock. It started to get personal. Come on, if you think you're hard enough. But, after an hour, my arms were like jelly. I turned the machine off, but for a while I kept bouncing. My vertical hold on the world took time to adjust, like stepping ashore after days at sea, trying to get your land-legs. Ian came over to inspect the damage to me and the rock. The granite had fared the better. There wasn't even a hole; just a series of grazes to show for an hour's work. We had to make a channel five feet long, 12 inches wide and 18 inches deep. Fat chance.

"Dynamite," another local expert had suggested. "Dynamite, *mais doucement.*"

I couldn't reconcile dynamite with gentleness. There was a story in the village about an impatient builder using dynamite on a job. He broke windows and shook old walls, before disappearing without trace, leaving the mess for someone else.

"A drill might be better than a hammer," said Ian. Better than dynamite anyway.

We went back to the hire shop to swap the hammer for a drill, which the man in the shop swore, on his mother's life, would be perfect for the job. The drill hummed. A blessed relief from the bouncing. Then, as the friction between steel bit and granite raised the temperature, the hum became a scream, then a squeal, then a screech. Dogs howled in sympathy. I imagine throughout the village, people woke from their siesta with their teeth on edge, and buried their heads under pillows. But the drill was easier to handle. This time I could concentrate the pressure precisely at one spot. I applied myself for an hour. We had penetrated ¼ inch. The drill went back to the hire shop. The man who had staked his life, and his mother's life, on his tools, accepted their failure with a phlegmatic shrug.

Over a pot of Assam tea, Ian's synapses began to pop.

"Heat," he said.

"Just wait 'til August," I replied. My synapses were still anaesthetised by hammering and drilling.

"No. Flame. Fire. And cold water." And he added, "The Egyptians did it; for the pyramid stones."

I gave him a sideways look.

He said, "Let's give it a go. We've got nothing to lose," and went in search of the blowtorch.

It worked. We pointed the flame at the stone for five minutes and then threw a jar of cold water at it. A flake of granite, like a flint arrowhead split violently, with a crack like a rifle shot. It flew across the courtyard and ricocheted off a lintel 20 feet away. Luckily neither of us was blinded or needed shrapnel removing from our fleshy parts. It worked, but it might kill us in the process.

We were just about to call it a day and open the pastis, when Rico arrived.

"How's the work going?" he asked looking around for holes in the rock.

"It's not," we said and explained the problems.

"You're working like women!" he said in disgust, throwing out his chest. "I know what you want. Wait there."

He shot off, and came back with a sledgehammer, its handle four feet long.

"This will do the job." he said. "Watch, and learn."

He planted himself on the granite, legs wide apart. Spitting on his hands, he lifted the hammer over his head and smashed it down on the rock. It bounced, and accelerated back over his head like something from a Popeye cartoon. It had him staggering backwards off-balance. We grabbed him before he fell and he shrugged us away.

"*Merde!*" he cried. "That's *roche froid!* You'll never shift that!" He went home to supper.

At the end of the first day we had the comfort of knowing that we'd made a start. We had a hole ¼ inch deep, some scratches and a granite arrowhead. Including the sledgehammer, we'd discounted four ways of doing the job. With a belly full of pasta and pastis, I went to sleep that night aware of every muscle and joint in my body. But part of my brain didn't rest; it applied itself to the problem in hand. When I opened my eyes next morning, the solution was obvious. Cut it.

Two coffees later as I was getting into my work boots, Ian and Ann arrived. "We'll cut it." Ian said. Part of his brain hadn't slept either.

FLUSHING OUT SOME LOCAL HISTORY

My angle-grinder is a monster machine; heavy, unwieldy and powerful. Ian's wrist is delicate, plated and pinned from a wild party injury. We wouldn't be able to take it in turns with the angle-grinder. This was all down to me. Our plan was to cut grooves an inch deep, an inch apart, two at a time, then to hammer steel chisels into the grooves. The rock should split from itself along the length and depth of the cut. And so on until we had a channel five feet by 12 inches by 18 inches. That was the theory. We'd discounted another method using wooden wedges, soaking them until the expanding wood split the rock. According to Ian this was another ancient Egyptian technique. But it sounded slow and unpredictable and the Egyptians had almost killed me yesterday. On balance I trusted the steel chisels more.

It was long, hard, hot and dusty work. Bent double like a potato picker, a vicious awkward machine at arm's length and trying to be accurate, my hamstrings twanged and my back threatened to seize. I remembered someone telling me that, at our age, being in pain is how you know you're alive. For a couple of hours I felt very, very alive. But, the relief at finding a solution that didn't involve high explosives or heavy plant was energizing, and I made good progress. At the same time, Ian was squatting over his trench in the earthy part of the courtyard. Using a garden trowel he was tunnelling towards me, and already had a trench two feet deep and six feet long. Separated earth and stones were piled up on either side. We stopped for a break, and looked at each other for the first time since we'd started. We were both covered in the thick white dust I was producing. He wasn't going home with much of a tan. As we sat there looking like Third World convicts serving hard labour, I was feeling guilty. This was, after all, his annual holiday. I asked if there wasn't something else he'd rather be doing. Building a bridge over the River Kwai, for example; or escaping from Devil's Island? The courtyard wasn't a pleasant place to be, so the girls went shopping to keep our supplies of carbohydrate topped up. Ian and I carried on, determined to make this second day more productive than the first. When our respective channels were about a yard apart, it was clear they weren't going to meet exactly. "Don't worry, it's easy going here. I'll just

EN GARD

widen my bit. It'll be right as rain," called Ian.

"Great. I'll just take this down another few inches, and swallow a bit more dust." Within moments I heard him shout. "I think you should take a look at this, kid." My first thought was that he'd hit more bedrock and my heart sank. I looked down into the dark earth and muddy stones and it took a second or two to focus on the brown segment of skull. Ian knew immediately, and seeing the distinctive curve of bone, so did I. It was human. With a tiny re-pointing trowel, Ian probed sideways and soon found the clavicle and some metatarsals. I found a bucket to put them in. For some reason we didn't think about calling the police. If it had happened in the back garden in Brighton, it would have been the first thing we did.

"Let's leave it until the girls get back," I said. They shouldn't miss out on any of this and I didn't know how much more skeleton there was.

When they arrived, Ann and Sandy stared into the bucket, and then at us.

"That's human, isn't it?" they said.

We were all quite calm. No thoughts of ghosts or uneasy spirits. It was clearly not a fresh skeleton, the bones were dark and crumbly. The region is historically rich; it could date back to the Roman occupation. Ian preferred to think it was Neolithic. We felt protective and curious in equal measure. What was the best thing to do? A pastis would help, to clear the dust in our throats and our thoughts on the bones, which by now my brother had christened 'Grunt'.

Gabby arrived and saw us gawping into the bucket.

"What's that?" he asked.

"Bones," I said. "A man's bones."

He didn't believe me. He likes a practical joke himself, and expects to be caught in return, once in a while. When he saw I was serious he didn't wait around. Most of the village would know within the hour.

UGLY RUMOURS

ALEX, OUR OTHER neighbour, is a doctor. I lay in wait for him the next morning, to get confirmation of what we knew, in our bones, was true. '*Oui*, Alistair, they are human."

"What now Alex?"

Shining from his eyes was the Frenchman's strong belief in personal responsibility, liberty and disregard for rules and regulations.

"It's not for me to say, Alistair. There are some who might dispose of these bones a very long way from here. Or they would put them back where they found them, and say nothing. Some might take them to the *gendarmerie*. Or call the archaeologists from Montpellier. *Alors*..." he shrugged deeply and gave me a wry smile. "*Au revoir! Bonne journée!*" and he was gone, leaving us to it.

Above all we had work to do. To finish it we need not disturb Grunt any further. The bones could rest in the bucket for the moment. Leaving us lunch, Ann and Sandy escaped the quarry/graveyard, and went to research tiles for floors in the house. Throughout the day, Chinese whispers from the village came back to us via Gabby. There were plenty of ideas about Grunt's real identity. In the late afternoon the plot thickened. Someone wanted to speak to me urgently in the neighbour's kitchen.

Sitting at the wooden table was a man I recognised, but could not place. We shook hands. No introductions, so we had definitely met before. Lola poured us pastis and then discreetly left. The man politely enquired about my health and my family's health. He complained about the weather and his liver. How was the work on the house? He had heard we'd made an interesting discovery.

"Do you know how it is in France?" he asked, "No? Let me explain. Any dealings with bureaucracy always leads to trouble.

The state thinks it has the right to know everything. It looks under every bed, in all the dark corners, into your past," he paused for effect, "and who among us can stand such examination? Being as we are, flawed and weak."

He poured us both another pastis, and I was intrigued to know what he was on about. Kitchen-table philosophy isn't that unusual in France, but he'd lost me. He continued, "Of course, it is possible to avoid all the unpleasantness. You say nothing – you are among friends here. What nobody knows, nobody knows." He put his finger to his lips and went on, "But if anybody knows, monsieur, anybody at all, then I am afraid that it is in-ev-it-able, that the Government in Paris –" he simulated spitting, at the thought "– will arrive. Teams of archaeologists will be at your gates within days. You will be forbidden access to your beautiful house for months, perhaps years, perhaps forever, while they make their investigations. It is like this with the protection of French culture, and the Napoleonic code." He was leaning so close I could smell his aftershave. This man was trying to frighten me. He obviously wanted me to keep my mouth shut. Who the Hell was he? Where did I know him from? Declining another pastis, I made my excuses and left, feeling edgy and bullied.

"Well?" asked Ian when I got home.

"We're taking the bones to the *gendarmes* first thing in the morning." I said. "Someone's just tried to warn me off, and I don't like it."

Among all the theories that Gabby had relayed to us earlier, were two stories of missing persons. A cantankerous old lady in the 1950s and the wife of a philanderer in the 1970s. Gabby had been quick to point out that the philanderer once lived in our house. Now, as I sat discussing with Ian all the possibilities about the skeleton, from Neanderthal gored by a woolly mammoth or Roman legionnaire struck down with typhus, to French Resistance or German spy, I remembered who the strange visitor was. The son of the philanderer. He had lost his inheritance – including our house – because of his father's bad debts. Lola had told us the sad story, and how the wife had left, fed up with the poverty as well as the infidelity. Surely the son didn't believe our bones were his mother, and that his father was a murderer? The old man still lived in a local town. Was all that stuff, about rampant archaeologists and the Napoleonic code, a ruse to protect his father's name? This complicated things. I didn't want to be responsible for sending an old man to jail in his eighties. The girls came back and we talked things through. In the end, we more or less agreed that the bones had to be declared. They were public knowledge. We felt sure they were too old to be missing women from the 50s and 70s. Village gossip is one thing but murder is rare. We didn't think our skeleton would lead to any arrests.

Next morning we rinsed the bones and put them in a new plastic washing-up bowl. When you dig a garden in England, you always find blue and white porcelain; here it is green and yellow earthenware. The shards we found alongside Grunt we included in the bowl; they might help in dating him.

It was after eleven when we arrived at the part-time gendarmerie. We rang the bell, the shutters opened, and a bored voice asked what our business was.

"I've found these," I said, holding-up the bowl. The shutters closed and he came down to unlock the gates, tucking in his shirt. Seeing what we had, he waved us inside. The expression on his face said "there goes my lunch". He took his time finding the paperwork to deal with human-remains-found-by-an-Englishman-digging-sewer-trenches, and we answered the catch-all questions. When asked if we could carry on digging, he shrugged, and didn't have an opinion either way. He didn't exactly say "don't leave town", but we gathered we shouldn't. We left hoping the world wasn't about to collapse around our ears.

A couple of days later he appeared at the house with our bowl and bones. They were more than 100 years old and, as far as the *gendarmes* were concerned, beyond investigation, beyond interest. They were not a thousand years old; we could rest easy that archaeologists wouldn't descend, expel us and take over the house for years. Now there were two choices. The mayor could arrange a pauper's grave in the local cemetery, or it would be acceptable for us to put the bones back where we found them. We got the distinct impression that, from the point of view of cost and paperwork, we should opt for the latter. We did. Wrapping the bones in clean linen, we put them back in the courtyard. Wishing them peace at last, we toasted them in pastis. They're marked by a large flat stone, and, when the place is no longer a building site, we'll plant something on the spot.

The most likely explanation for the skeleton being there is the religious wars. Protestants were not allowed to bury their dead in Catholic cemeteries. If the family had no spare land for a mausoleum, it was quite usual to bury the body under the floor in the house, marking the doorway with a cross. As we dug further towards the gate, we discovered cornerstones from an ancient wall. It would make sense then, that the body was once in a room and not open ground.

What happened to the old lady and the cuckolded wife remains a mystery for now.

TOAD IN THE HOLE

GRUNT LAID TO rest, we went back to plumbing. There were lengths of PVC tubing to buy, in so many different diameters, it was more like building a church organ than laying sewer pipes. 125mm for the main drain, 100mm for the loos, 50mm for sinks, 40mm for sinks, 32mm for washing machines. Handel's Messiah! Hallelujah! Let's go! The last practical consideration and calculation was the descent for the pipes. Without going into gory detail, if the run was too shallow nothing would move; too steep and water would rush away leaving solid matter behind. Fastidiously we measured every metre with a spirit level, and, when we achieved the recommended 35 to 50mm fall over the metre, we glued. And then we set off to buy a proper loo.

Bricomarché and Mr Bricolage had a display of toilets in white and all the usual insipid and swampy colours. No-one could explain why one toilet, which looked fine to us, was ten times more expensive than another, which also looked fine. Bog-standard, surely. Sandy remembered a specialist shop in a town close by, maybe we could learn more there. The shop was impressive; huge plate glass windows and divided inside into bathroom set-pieces. How many different ways are there to arrange a bath, a loo and a basin? Shelves of nuts, bolts and washers, as well as accessories from marble soap dishes to gold dolphin taps; something for everyone's taste. But there was also something in the shop to no-one's taste. As we moved among the displays, trying handles and chains, flushes and seats and lids, we came to a handsome pot-bellied unit. We liked everything about it, including the price, until we lifted the lid. Shocking, in this classy, pristine environment, was a huge turd stuck to the dry interior of the bowl. The display was right in front of the plate glass windows. We left wondering when, and how, it could have happened – in full view of the street and the bus-stop outside. And why? Then, as now, I

EN GARD

don't know the French for 'Monsieur, there's a turd in your toilet-bowl' so we didn't mention anything. We didn't buy anything either. We found, elsewhere, a plain old-fashioned white loo, which we assembled in the ground floor room. The final nightmare was knocking a hole in the wall to connect up. In the wee small hours, when suicides are at their highest, I had imagined the holes would bring the house tumbling down, like a 'château des cartes'. It wasn't easy going. The walls are well built. The mixture of large and small stones leaves no clear passage, however you make the hole. It was slow, knee-numbing work, but nothing fell down. We joined the toilet to the pipes outside, ran copper tubing to the cistern and then, for the second time in a month, our well-being relied on a sheet or two of moving toilet tissue. We scrunched up some quilted pink, and flushed it away. Running to the end of the main pipe, seconds later we were rewarded with a wad of soggy paper sitting in our trench. Sandy wanted to experiment further using a packet of merleuz sausages, 'to make it more realistic', but I put my foot down. Now we had to be joined to the main drain in the road, just a couple of metres away, and that was out of our hands.

Dominic, the young mayor, had stopped by the day before. He took a pastis and cast his eyes over the work we'd done. The courtyard looked like a WW1 battlefield; grey PVC tubing glued and weighted with stones, piles of dirt and rock either side of trenches waiting to be refilled. Doing it ourselves in the courtyard was fine, he said, but at the gates the professionals must take over. Not that he doubted we could do the work. Non, non, non. It was a question of insurance, he hoped we understood. There were costs to be incurred too. For the privilege of joining the village sewers we must pay 917 euros, including tax. On top of this, there would be the bill from the contractor, to dig up the road, do the pipe work and repair the road afterwards. There was a list of approved contractors in the mayor's office. If we would like to drop in, we could pay the 917 euros at the same time. When we called to get the list, it had one name on it. It was a large local building company; the head of which, it transpired, was the mayor of a village not too far away. We got our estimate, 1046 euros, for two metres

TOAD IN THE HOLE

of work; using all the proper plant and equipment, it would probably take them a morning. We couldn't resist doing a calculation. For them to have done all the really hard work in the courtyard – not much change out of 25,000 euros we thought. Impatient to have our flushing loo, we accepted the estimate, and asked when the work would start. Friday. Definitely. If not Friday, then Tuesday. Definitely. Or Thursday at the latest.

At 8a.m. on Thursday they arrived; two men with a mechanical digger leaking hydraulic fluid over the road. They had sandwiches and coffee for their morning break, which they took separately without speaking. In France, unless you are self-employed you don't work more than 35 hours a week. This is adhered to and calculated to the milli-second. They could not find the main drain, despite having two manhole covers to line up with. There was the one at the bottom of the lane,which we had found with the local expert, and another, which he had wrongly identified, around the corner. We pointed this out and they tried again. Then there was the question of how deep. If there existed a plan of the village system, they obviously didn't have it. Professionals, my eye. Trench dug and lined up with our pipes, they then discovered they had a junction box with the wrong configuration of exits. Our pipes were 18ins down and the mains were 6ft down. Instead of changing the box, they crudely cut extra holes – borrowing our drill and jigsaw to do it. They cobbled everything together with chicken wire and plastic bags, which we also provided. Professionals, my arse. Luckily all contracted work is guaranteed for 10 years in France. The plastic bags may last that long, but I don't know about the chicken wire. They finished as the village clock struck midday, lunchtime. We didn't see them again for five weeks, when they came back to resurface the road. We didn't care: 18 months into the restoration, we no longer had to pee in the wind and rain. Not once since have I come out of the 'makeshift' bathroom without smiling. 'Everything in the house should be beautiful or useful' is Sandy's guiding principle. To me, the loo is both.

For sale: One Porta-potti; two previous, grateful users.

There is a postscript. Because the courtyard trenches were shallow, we wanted to protect the pipes in the channels by supporting them with sand. Two tons arrived, and wheelbarrow by wheelbarrow we emptied it around the PVC tubes and stamped it down wearing wide flip-flops. We stopped work because it started to rain. It didn't stop raining for 48 hours. Gardoise rain, relentless and heavy. Our trenches were man-made riverbeds. The water cascading off roofs found them a path of least resistance, out of the courtyard and into the street. It carried away almost every grain of sand we'd laid down. There was a small beach at the end of the lane. When the rain finally ceased, we replaced the sand with gritty soil, which hasn't budged in the storms since.

 A woman in the village, who is converting stables into *gîtes*, called on us last week. Could she ask my advice about installing drains in bedrock? Of course, Madame. My pleasure. I'll keep quiet about the sand.

June 2003
Life is just a jar of cherries –
soaked in rum if you're lucky

Dearest Den
Writing this with bright red hands, like a washerwoman. Nails, whorls and lifeline all stained scarlet with cherry juice. Wonder if 'caught red handed' comes from scrumping cherries.

Always thought beetroot was the strongest dye known to man, but cherries must be close second. We're making rumptopfs – wide-neck bottling jars filled with fruits as they come in season, and covered in sugar and rum. By Christmas it is ready to eat, and the liqueur will soften your edges nicely. You won't care what presents you get.

Cherries are a big crop here. When the Iraq war started, the local paper ignored it, favouring news of a bumper harvest. Every mile along the road, a child or granny sits under a parasol with a stall of fruit. We made ourselves ill the first year, driving along with a bagful on our laps and spitting stones out of the windows. But this year they are the first layer in our rumptopfs, followed soon by strawberries and raspberries, then redcurrants, peaches and plums. Roll on Christmas.

Both been a bit sickly, our usual cast-iron digestions bordering on incontinence. A whole series of chemical reactions keeping us close to plumbing. We think it might be eggs, which we buy all over the place – the baker, the fish van, markets and supermarkets and from the side of the road. Not much quality control. Even had a couple of 'illegal' double-yolkers from the market, which is still like finding buried treasure even at our age.

Talking of buried treasure, while we were feeling low and not up to much hard work, Scotty wanted to try water-divining. No hazel wands to hand, so he made do with a metal coat-hanger. He can do it. He has the gift. Once he started he couldn't stop, and we ended up in the neighbour's house, trying to find the underground spring that floods them in heavy rains. A bit suspiciously it seemed to be under the washing

EN GARD

machine. But, when we moved it, there was a stone plug in the floor with a metal handle. Underneath, a vast vaulted and tiled water cistern, who knows how old. The gypsies got very excited and thought they had found a 'source', another Perrier. Like Butch Cassidy, they keep having ideas. The water tasted sweet enough, but was only a couple of feet deep. They would have to wait for rain. The 'source' might be a bit unreliable. The kids were freaked by divining, and thought it was magic and the Devil's work. They both dropped the hanger and ran when it moved in their hands. Scotty made a brave attempt at explaining electromagnetic fields, but they preferred the idea of magic. Our fossil collection is growing. The latest has spent a few years as a doorstop. Up against a nailed-up door in a dark corner, we've only just seen that it isn't just a lump of rock. Shaped like an elephant's trunk, shorter and thicker with heavy ridges around it. We hear Madame Favede has about a dozen of them propping-up her washing line. What can they be – mammoth's ribs?

The season of Sunday 'fairs' has started in Uzès. In the open air, under the shade of the plane trees in the market square, they are a good crowd-puller. Kicking off with a tortoise fair, with animals from Madagascar to Greece; some the size of a watch face, others big as boulders. They're not for sale – it's a conservation/information day – but you can buy tortoise-shaped things. Earrings, fridge magnets, bookmarks. You can definitely spend money. Later in the summer it's more artisanal and commercial. Silk, wood, ceramics – breathtaking work at breathtaking prices. Leave your money at home, and then it is just a good way to walk off Sunday lunch.

We think your furniture reclamation is a brilliant idea. Lots of early morning starts for the garage sales and late-night skip raids... Wished you were here when the woodman moved house; he left outside for any-one to help themselves – a pine meat safe, cast-iron garden bench with a rotten wood seat, witches' cauldron planted with bulbs, a deckchair and a wonky hat stand, as well as a bike and plastic tat. All disappeared by the time I went back for the meat safe; I never learn.

Hope the present arrives in time for your birthday; it's a really ugly yellow and brown parcel but don't be put off...

Have a great day, with Longshanks and Sushi, all our love
Sandy & Scotty

PAYMENT BY PHEASANT

IN THE LONG, hot summer of 2003, Rico had been going AWOL three or four times a week. Lola's suspicion was a mistress – *'une petite cherie'* tucked away in town. In fact he was having a full-blown existential, mid-life crisis – though he didn't know what existentialism was and his whole life was a series of crises.

Lola's ongoing mystery illness meant she had stopped work. Rico had to give up the fanciful and potentially lucrative dalliance with horse-training, to go out and find some way to put *baguettes* and pastis on the table. She stopped being the breadwinner, a powerful position which she loved, and he had taken some control back, a position which terrified and intoxicated him in equal measure. The friction was producing lots of fireworks, tears and broken glass.

One evening Lola came to me and asked me to talk to Rico. I said I wouldn't talk to him, but I'd listen if he wanted to talk to me. Adding that he might not be ready yet, and that things might get worse before they got better. Speaking from experience.

I'd seen Rico a couple of times in Uzès, leaning on bars in the middle of the day, with pastis for company. Once I waved when he looked in my direction but he'd seen nothing, focused on some inner misery. "Pissed," I thought, but as I got closer I could see he was almost in shock – frozen and round-shouldered, a Gitane burning down to its filter, eyes fixed in a thousand-yard stare. I backed away. Not what Lola would want me to do, but he was best left alone for now. What could I say to change the facts? He had borrowed heavily to set himself up in a rendering business – spraying new villas in ice cream colours or repairing old façades. Hours were spent chatting up clients in bars, alcohol lubricating the deals. The work was there and he was undercutting everyone on price, but his second-hand machinery kept breaking down. He had dissatisfied customers and bills to pay, as well as horses to feed and a sick wife. And, of course, he wasn't getting any younger, and a man in the shit seldom has many friends. Half a dozen times he phoned from Uzès just before he passed out, to say he would sleep in the car until he could drive home safely. He misjudged it once and we had to haul his car out of a ditch.

The pressure was building. Social and business drinking was out of control and he was mean and aggressive, even to his kids. He and Lola were like brittle strangers when they weren't hurling abuse.

Weeks went by and things didn't improve. Then they got much worse.

At two o'clock one morning, dog-tired after a day's roofing, Sandy shook me awake. The kids from next door were hammering on the gates and shouting my name.

"What's the matter?" I asked through a yawn as I opened the door. All three of the youngest children were in their pyjamas, trembling, their eyes like bush-babies'.

"Alistair, please come quickly! Papa has gone berserk!"

"I'm coming. Let me get dressed."

"Hurry. Please hurry."

Sandy and I got into our work-clothes and unlocked the gates. The kids threw themselves at us, arms locked around our legs. They were all badly shaken. The 14-year-old asked me for a cigarette.

"What's going on?' I demanded.

They didn't really know. When the screaming and shouting and fighting got too much, they'd run away. To somewhere they'd always felt safe – our garage.

Suddenly Lola hurtled into the street, barefoot and looking over her shoulder, panting and voice trembling.

"Alistair – he's going to kill us all and then kill himself!"

While Sandy took Lola and the kids into the garage, thinking calming English thoughts of tea, I set off into the neighbours' house. I knew Rico had a fine selection of hunting knives and three shotguns to choose from to carry out his threat. Everything felt out of control and dangerous and I didn't know what I was going to find inside. I must have been scared, but I went into the house calling Rico's name and following the sounds of fighting. Going from room to room, the thought occurred that the only way out was getting farther and farther behind me.

Back in the garage the kids climbed into our bed, fighting over who would have 'Alistair's side'. Lola chain-smoked and told Sandy that Rico had given her a slap. Of course, she would take the kids and go; any woman who stayed when she'd been beaten deserves everything she gets. Whipping herself into a frenzy, and winding herself up again.

In the house behind the door to the last bedroom, I could hear a violent struggle, words spoken through gritted teeth and incoherent drunken ranting. I called Rico's name out loudly and went into the room. Rico and Toni were locked together in a wrestle. The single, unshaded bulb was swinging, casting a strange light on the struggle. Rico looked manic. His eyes were raw and sunken and there was dried snot and spittle on his face and fresh spit bubbling out of his mouth, like a man in a grand mal seizure. He was roaring and wailing, dragging Toni across the room and reaching for the gun-rack on the wall. Toni had one arm around Rico's neck and was pulling him back from the guns, struggling to keep his balance.

"Get him down on the bed!" I said and added my weight to the tussle.

The tiring strength of one drunk against the power of two sober men wasn't enough to keep him on his feet to grab a gun. We tumbled in a heap on the old bed which sagged and groaned. It took Toni and me a few seconds to work out who would grab which flailing part of Rico to subdue him, and in that time he hit us both in the face. He was soaked in sweat and the sweat stank of pastis.

If he couldn't move, Rico could still wail and roar. He threatened to kill me too, but that, at least, sounded like a man talking. The screams and wails were chilling and inhuman. Demonic.

In a voice sloppy and cloyed with booze he began to describe with passion the rage that was eating him, stuck in his throat and choking him. He couldn't breathe. He changed his mind – he didn't want to kill me, and he begged me to go so that he wouldn't have to. He lay back on the bed, exhausted. Toni and I kept our hold on him but relaxed it.

Just as he seemed calm enough to sleep it off, Lola burst into the room with Sandy holding onto her for dear life. Like a harpie, Lola lunged towards Rico screaming abuse at him, his weakness and his uselessness, her hoarse bitching rattle, like gunfire, cutting through the progress we'd made and refuelling Rico's angst. He screamed that she was destroying him.

"Lola!" Sandy shouted "Lola, please leave it – come back to the kids. They're frightened." Appeals to her motherliness weren't the answer.

"Lola," I said. "Sod off. You're making things worse!"

She shut up and Sandy hauled her out of the room. Rico collapsed and we let him ramble, stroking his hair and his face like a child. His frenzy re-erupted once or twice but with less energy, and then he lay still. Alcohol and tiredness were slowly knocking him out, and I told Toni I'd wait in the next room, leaving father and son together.

I could still hear them talking and Rico was sobbing. He was crying for himself, weeping with self-pity. Why? Why? Why? Repeated over and over.

In a while they emerged quietly from the bedroom and that seemed like a good time for me to go.

"Put him under a shower," I suggested, "and while he's there make sure all those guns are unloaded. Hide the knives, too."

In the street I tried to make Lola understand that she should know when to back off. She should let the anger seep away this time. Her eyes were defiant and still burning and she gave me no such assurances. Gathering up the kids, fast asleep in our bed, she went home and left us to hope she'd do nothing to inflame Rico.

Sandy and I sat in bed and went over our two stories. It was then I found out that Rico might have hit Lola. Sandy wasn't convinced and thought it might have been talked up to get some sympathy. I hoped she was right – it wouldn't have helped any peace-making or keeping if it was true.

We'd just gone back to sleep when there was another knock at the gates.

"Oh no," groaned Sandy. "Don't go, Scotty." She thought I'd

done my duty and then some.

"What is it?" I shouted.

It was Gabby and he sounded almost cheerful. "Papa wants a word with you."

"Better go," I said.

I felt vaguely apprehensive climbing the terrace steps. Rico was waiting at the top, swaying gently, his eyes wet and unfocused. He put his hands on my shoulders, and I half expected a knee in the groin. In its place he gave me a bear-hug and whispered, "Alistair, you are family." It sounded like a curse.

"Come," he said, and he bounced off the wall and door-frame into the kitchen. Surely he wasn't going to offer me a pastis. No, instead he opened the freezer door and took out a frozen pheasant. Like everything he shoots, it had gone into the freezer head, feathers, feet and all. The ice crystals made the blue and green plumage iridescent, the neck frozen stiff at a right angle. He held it out to me by its ugly feet.

"Here. For you. Take it. Thank you."

Tears filled his eyes. I took it and went home, shaking my head the whole way. Opening the garage door, I carried it out in front of me, like a bunch of flowers.

"I'm really glad you're here – or you might not have believed this," I said.

"What in the name of God..?" asked Sandy.

"It's wages for tonight's work."

For weeks the pheasant sat in the freezer, the big claws scratching and snagging as we reached past for something. Neither of us fancied plucking it, and Lola didn't take the hint and do it for us.

The resolution came after a storm and a long power cut – when we could legitimately throw it out. On health grounds.

St Lydia's Day, Aug 2003
also Fête du Jasmin in Grasse & Fête du Raisins in Frejus – nothing there for me to celebrate especially, but having a glass of red anyway...

Dear Jean & Dick,
   All quiet here, almost peaceful, though not exactly silent. The sainted World Service coming and going in the background, with its exotic correspondents – Demeter Luthera and Damian Grammaticus – covering everything from face transplants to miracle honey to basketball results to demonic possession and Lebanese folk music. How did we ever live without it? Out here in the courtyard about ten thousand bees in the linden tree humming like distant motorway traffic, assorted birds cackling and bickering and a very camp pigeon oooooooing on the roof.
   Being Sunday we half expect visitors, and today they were total strangers – to us, if not to the house. A man in his fifties with two grown children. He spent school holidays here with his aunt and uncle, and he took us on a guided tour with his forty-year-old memories. The son and daughter indulgent and bemused; us enjoying the history lesson.
   He said the strange hole in the wall on the outside stairs used to house a chicken. Close to the kitchen door for collecting the eggs. But it had been a 'guard' chicken too. Better than any Doberman, ready to peck your eyes out, as you ran up the stairs. He had been terrified.
   The rich yellow colour on some walls was a white emulsion – the only paint available for years after the war – mixed with chicken shit. All the animals had more than one use. The paint is still a deep egg-yolk yellow after all this time. Those big iron hooks in the ceilings that we imagined were for hanging hams and 'boudins noirs' were a bit more grisly. Pig and sheep had hung there for butchering. Blood collected in pails which he carried for his aunt, careful not to spill a drop. The swinging carcasses had given him nightmares. We said it didn't sound like much of a hol-

ST LYDIA'S DAY

iday, and his children wrinkled their noses.

A horse slept in our bathroom and two cows in the cobbled room next-door. The two spaces formed by stoning up part of the big arch were for a suckling sow and the boar. Chickens roosted above their heads. Precarious life for the birds, if pigs will eat anything.

The long branches on wires hanging from attic rafters, like communal swings, were for drying tobacco, which uncle grew for his own use in a clay pipe.

We dragged out our collection of mildewy photos, school reports and payslips which we've found, along with a notebook in a child's hand, of matches and scores from inter-village football. Our village beat St Marcel 4-3 one January a long time ago, when there were still enough village boys to make up a team. He looked through it all, but couldn't put names to old faces or faces to the names. He's promised to come back with photos of his own and we look forward to it. Hope he comes on his own; I think the son and daughter would rather have gone for a MacDonald's.

Got lost during the week. Out in the garrigue, we forgot all our jungle-craft and common or garden sense, trying to find some old stone buildings we had stumbled across once before. There's a romantic story about them being hiding places in the religious wars and more recently for the Resistance. Some no more than a place to squat down, others big enough for a horse and cart. We soon got lost in thickets of holly, oak and brambles. Successful hideouts. When it was too dense to go forward we turned back and that was twice as dense. All the plants were vicious, all the insects stingers and we had one bottle of water, no warm clothes and sunset in about an hour. Only by chance, we came into a wide clearing, part of an old terracing system and up quite high. It gave us a view of where we wanted to be, and only about a square mile of sharp thorns, prickly leaves and biting bugs away. God looks after fools, and after about ten minutes we found a hunters' path, rough and steep, but going in the right direction. We stopped for a drink and saw a movement ahead on the path. A wild boar and five piglets rooting about, tossing clumps of soil in the air. Their eyesight is bad, but we were surprised they couldn't smell our sweat or hear us puffing and panting. They snuffled about for a few more minutes and then ploughed off into the bushes. We've heard that a wild boar with piglets will attack to protect them, so we used up lots of luck that day.

EN GARD

Big feast of flowers in the courtyard over the last few days – the lilies all out together fighting for your olfactory lobes, and the 'yellow' wall with the honeysuckle and trumpets of Jericho and a rose climber called 'Teasing Georgia' attracting butterflies and moths – like harlots' hankies some of them. An insect we can't identify, something between a bee and a hummingbird, going mad for the lavender. Keep hearing about all the wild life in the world not yet discovered, and think, some evenings, that most of it is here. I hope Dick will bring his paints if you come out next year. Not much lavender around us, just the odd field, but we have sunflowers to the horizon. Better to paint when they're past their best, otherwise they're a bit chocolate-box. When they dry out and brown off and birds peck out some seeds they are wonderful studies. Last summer in the heatwave the local lake dried completely. Sunflower seeds must have been carried by the wind and birds and lain dormant. When the water evaporated they came up out of the cracked mud and we had a lake of sunflowers, surrounded by bullrushes and some very confused ducks. If Dick likes Beth Chatto's gardens then he might like David Austin's, too. All roses, but nothing pearls and twin set about them; nothing too tidy. Big, ragged mop-head flowers with plenty of perfume – a bonus while you paint them.

Sitting here talking about flowers reminds me I should weed – which, like ironing, is only bearable after half a bottle of wine.

Love to you both,
Sandy and Alistair.

LISETTE'S TOMATO SALAD

LISETTE HAD her house as part of a divorce settlement over thirty years ago. She doesn't live in the village, but spends long summers here with her cat. She arrives with a battery of straw hats, and Swiss cheese and chocolate for her friends. Life in the village quickens while she's here. She opens a door you didn't even know was closed.

A go-between, a fence-mender, a bandager of knees. A fearless straight-talker with a heart the size of Saturn. A woodpecker stammer and a belly laugh that bounces off the stone walls. Queen of tomato salad makers.

Her house is in the middle of the village, and may be 15th century; walls like ramparts and bedrooms like monastic cells. The old communal bread oven takes up one room, and an engineer boyfriend built her a minstrels' gallery, out of the pages of the Brothers Grimm.

A few of us had supper in her courtyard one night; entertained by a family of hedgehogs in her compost heap, bleating like lambs. We were wiping our plates clean with bread, when there was a knock at the gate.

A man with a bicycle and a ghostly white dog asked where in the village he could sleep for the night. Not a bed; a quiet piece of flat grass for himself and his dog. He had tried the cemetery, but the road was too noisy. In the last week he had travelled down from Normandy, looking for work in the vineyards.

Monsieur Gouderch suggested level land by the Lion's Head fountain would be a good place to camp, and Lisette made him a midnight feast of goat's cheese, bread and melon, with a tin of catfood for the dog. We walked him down the street, pointed out the fountain, and wished him goodnight. We agreed it was a pity we had eaten all the tomato salad. It would have been good with his cheese.

EN GARD

The recipe:

Tomatoes; the uglier the better for flavour. If they look like Sid James, that's about right. It doesn't matter if they are slightly green. Allow two per person of the fist-sized ones. Three if the person has been roofing all day.

Olive oil: cold pressed extra virgin, the most expensive you can buy or afford. 'Robert' is a good French label. Opaque and nutty and peppery. Like khaki-green emulsion.

Garlic: sweet fat cloves of the violet Provençal garlic, if you can find it. How much is up to you, but be brave.

Basil, flat-leaf parsley and chives from pots on a warm windowsill.

Ground salt and pepper.

A big flat dish, so that the tomatoes can sit and swim in the flavours.

An hour before you want to eat, wash and slice the tomatoes. They should never be kept in the fridge. Tomato flavour improves with warmth. Cut them across, not up and down and vary the thicknesses. Arrange them on your dish. Chop most of the garlic into tiny pieces and crush the rest. Spread this over the tomatoes.

Smother the tomatoes with olive oil.

Chop up the herbs and don't be fussy about it. Sprinkle them over the dish.

A few grinds of black pepper, leaving the salt until just before eating.

Serve with a good mopping bread – *gros pain* or *pain à l'ancienne* or a white farmhouse.

And plenty of paper napkins.

October 19th, 2003
Harvest moon and howling dogs...

Sue,

It was lovely to get your long letter. Like chimney sweeps and lock-keepers, letter writers seem to be a dying breed. Telephones and e-mails are useful, but nothing like seeing that blue airmail envelope sitting in the box on the gate.

Here it is well and truly autumn, the hunting season. The French are out every weekend, hunting chestnuts, mushrooms and wild boar; the Dutch and English are house-hunting. It's also the smoky season. The fields are being burnt off, and the vine prunings make huge pyres. In the villages it is just cold enough, morning and evening, to light a wood-burning stove. Fastidious gardeners have billowing bonfires of leaves, which is bad news for hedgehogs. Even if the day has been hot, when the sun goes down, chunky cardigans come out. The three sisters have abandoned their seat under the mulberry tree until Spring; their canny cats keep warm sitting on the bonnets of newly parked cars. Wood deliveries have begun to appear outside gates; dry oak and elm by the cubic metre. Old hands buy cheaper green wood now and keep it to burn next winter. That's something we'll do next summer; it takes a couple of years to catch up.

Wood-stacking is one of my favourite chores; a wall of beautiful logs is worth the splinters, bruised knuckles, and a creaking back. While I'm stacking I often separate anything with an interesting shape or grain. I bury them low down in the pile, to be used last. One, like a map of Africa at one end – with cracks for the Nile and the Niger – is still there from last year. Maybe I should apply for an Arts Council grant. Alistair and I have different fire philosophies. I can't abide a smouldering black hole; it must be blazing all the time, rattling the flue. Alistair is happy with a few glowing embers, and not wasting wood. We sit for a long time in the evening in front of the stove, often without saying a word. 'Off with the fairies' my mother would have called it. Until a log will crack and break *the spell, and we remember we have to boil water for spaghetti. Firelight flickering on the ceiling is more soporific than a wagon-load of Peter Rabbit's lettuce.*

Over the summer we've been getting used to living together again – which we haven't done in an everyday did-you-remember-to-put-the-cat-out sort of way, for about two years. While I was coming for four days every second week, those four days were quite intense. We took great care never to argue or whinge, and always to part in a good mood; it had a honeymoon unreality about it. Now we can bicker about paint colours and who makes the first coffee, like everyone else.

Work progresses, as far as the heat, late deliveries and village social life allows. We enjoy sharing the courtyard with bats, rats and cats, a robin, swallowtails and lizards – with or without their tails – and with all the casual droppers-in for gossip, advice and pastis. I'm quite good at multi-tasking now, getting the cement mixer to what jam-makers call a 'rolling boil' while weeding the melon patch and making a vinaigrette.

Washing-day today; my hair and a sack of clothes. As we now have the use of an ancient top-loader in a neighbour's house, the sack of clothes isn't a problem. But my hair can be a bit of a workout; involving an assortment of buckets with hot, warm and cold water for all the rinses long hair needs. A shaved head sometimes seems like a very good idea. I dry my hair in the sun, so I spent that time sorting my stones. There are three holes in the walls to be repaired after doing the sewerage system. Golden rule of stone-wall building is 'one over two, two over one' and so I'm sorting by size and shape before I start the job. I've been patching all the walls where they need it, and I'm only really happy if, when I've finished, my stones look as if they've been there since 1807. Working with cement and rock, my hands are like sandpaper. Coarse grade, like a tiger's tongue. I have to use surgical gloves to put my tights on. I'm a bit shy about shaking hands too; lunging forward for the triple cheek kiss instead.

Great celebrations among the gypsy neighbours. The second son is betrothed. Tradition demands that he 'kidnaps' a gypsy girl and keeps her for two nights. This either has her father's approval or it doesn't. Either way, after the two nights, her virginity is symbolically lost – these days it probably really is – and the kidnapper must make an honest woman of her. They are betrothed. The boy next door has had non-gypsy girlfriends,

HARVEST MOON AND HOWLING DOGS

but they were too liberated for his parents' taste. His father told us that it was OK to sleep with 'gadjots', but not to marry them. At the betrothal party we'll be asked to put money towards a new caravan for the couple. It won't be quaint, wooden and horse drawn. More luxurious than our garage probably, and pulled by a Mercedes.

We are invited for drinks with Lisette tonight, so I'd better go and wash behind my ears and change into something not splattered with cement. Lisette wouldn't mind if I didn't. She's delightfully nutty, and wanders the village at all hours, in her nightdress, walking her cat. But, just because I live on the most beautiful building site in the world, standards don't have to fall too far...

I know your life is full to overflowing, and time with your boys is precious. I don't expect to hear from you regularly. Write when you can, however haphazardly, with news of your garden and weekends by the sea.

All good things,
Sandy

FIASCO de FOIE GRAS

IT WAS THE THIRD week of August, in the hottest summer since records began. Too hot to work, too hot to sleep, too hot to eat, too hot to speak. Sunflowers frazzling in the fields, grapes shrivelling on the vines, spit drying in your mouth. You would have sold an only son for a slice of ice-cold watermelon. And Lola was planning her stall for the Christmas market in the middle of December.

Her specialities were table decorations, centrepieces for Christmas dinner; confections of dried flowers and pine cones, gold and silver, red and green, somewhere between birds of Paradise and Ascot hats; and also baskets of local delicacies tied up with ribbons and bows. But this year she wanted to try something different, a real money-spinner – home-made *pâté de foie gras*.

This Christmas treat, apart from a few decorative peppercorns and bay leaves, is made entirely from a duck or goose liver. The liver is enlarged and engorged by force-feeding the bird, ramming a funnel down its throat and pouring maize and lard through it, until the bird swallows or chokes. The final fat content is truly frightening. When the liver is swollen to ten times its normal size, the bird is slaughtered and the livers go to make *pâté de foie gras*. Strictly taboo amongst most people we know, out of compassion for the animals and fear for their own cholesterol count.

In the countryside, it is still traditional for families to keep and fatten their own geese and to make their own *pâté*. Lola wasn't raising her own birds, but she had seen a special offer on raw duck *foie gras* in a local supermarket. She was going to get her sister-in-law's family recipe, and clean up at the Christmas market.

The next evening Lola and Rico came round for an *apéritif*. Lola carried an oven tray covered in hot toasted bread, smeared with butter and something smelling blissfully bad for you.

"Try this – you've never tasted anything like it before," she said;

FIASCO DE FOIE GRAS

Lola the Lorelei. She was right; it was an explosion of meaty perfume in our mouths, a sensual texture, a sexy flavour. We moaned with pleasure.

"What is it?" I asked. As if we didn't know.

"*Foie gras!* From my cousins in Cahors. Have another piece, Alistair have more – here." She picked up two slices and tried to put them both in my mouth. We had done it, we had broken the taboo; we were going to Hell.

"Isn't that good? You see why it costs so much?" said the Lorelei. Our mouths were too full to answer.

"Sandy," she said, pinching Sandy's arm – a habit which is going to get her a slap one day – "we should go to the supermarket tomorrow, before the special offer ends." I saw Sandy's eyes widen at the word 'we'.

Lola went on, "We should buy all they have. Go halves. You can learn to make *pâté de foie gras* – just like a real Frenchwoman! A real peasant!'"

Next morning she called for us early, anxious to be on the supermarket doorstep when it opened.

"Have you noticed anything?" said Sandy as we got out of the car.

"Only that the sun is barely over the horizon," I said, yawning.

"She hasn't brought her handbag," Sandy said, and twisted her mouth to one side. As a natural mimic Sandy had quickly acquired, by osmosis, by seeing it every day, a vocabulary of body language for all occasions. Facial expressions too. The twisted mouth could be many things depending on the context. Like "we've been had..."

Lola rushed straight to the freezer cabinet, where there were a few *foie gras* left.

"This was full yesterday," she said breathlessly. "Thank God we came before it's too late." The ten *foie gras* came to 80 euros. Lola did some gypsy mental arithmetic and calculated that we should make at least 500 euros profit on our home-made *pâté*.

Sandy twisted her mouth to one side again, to say "you're off your trolley".

"Might as well stock up on food, while we're here," I said, and so by the time we got to the checkout, the cart was quite full.

While we paid for everything, Lola went off to talk to someone she knew, and caught up with us as we reached the door.

"I'll keep this," she said snatching the till receipt, with its money-back credits, from Sandy's hand. "If you save enough of these, you can throw a party for almost nothing. I like to keep them for Christmas." Sandy's mouth slipped round to the side again. And so did mine.

In the car on the way home, Lola said we would sort out the money later. At the house, she put the *foie gras* in her freezer, and we didn't hear any more about them, or the money, for two months.

At the start of November, the shops began to fill with Christmas stock and posters for the Christmas market appeared.

"I wonder when the *foie gras* 'factory' is going into production," said Sandy. "We don't have much time left." I had forgotten all about it.

"Oh yes," I said. "Five hundred euros profit – very handy for Christmas!" Sandy cornered Lola the next day.

"Yes, yes, we must do it. Time flies," she agreed. "We'll do it while the kids are at school. I will defrost them and we can do it on Thursday."

"What else do we need? Do we have enough jars?" asked Sandy.

"I've got dozens somewhere," said Lola vaguely, "but no seals."

"O.K. I bought some new jars. 16 – is that enough?"

"Perfect. I'll call my sister-in-law for the recipe tonight, and we'll do it this week."

"I'll tell Alistair I'm working in the *foie gras* 'factory' and can't mix cement on Thursday."

On Wednesday Sandy went to check that all the *foie gras* were out of the freezer.

"*Merde!*" cried Lola, " I completely forgot. I'll do it now." Before she left home the next morning, Sandy scrubbed her hands until they stung, cleaned and cut her fingernails and tied her hair back in a scarf. She chose a freshly washed work shirt that reached past her knees, in lieu of an apron.

"Do you think this will get me past 'Environmental Health', if they come calling?" she asked. In Lola's kitchen, the table was spread with the defrosted raw *foie gras*. Ten slabs of pure fat, saffron yellow, with a slight sheen, about the size of kippers. The Kilner jars were put through the dishwasher to be sterilised. Lola handed Sandy a filleting knife; its edge keen enough to shave with. She demonstrated this by shaving with it; she cut some fine hairs from her forearm, and told Sandy to be careful. They spent the next hour taking out the tough veins inside the livers, which would turn gristly if left in during cooking. The texture of the flesh, after freezing, was fragile and it fell apart in their hands. Searching for every shred of vein was like picking out grains of salt from a bowl of jelly. Lola assembled a selection of red and green peppercorns and bay leaves, and took the jars out of the dishwasher to cool.

"My mother was there when I rang my sister-in-law – and of course she had to get involved," said Lola, over a cigarette, and she rolled her eyes heavenward. Relations are very cool between her and her mother, who never visits or buys birthday presents for the kids. Lola was her late father's favourite, and in families some jealousies are never resolved.

"She told me that we should add cognac to the *foie gras* before we seal it. What do you think? I don't know if I trust her. She might say that just to ruin it for me."

"What did your sister-in-law think about the idea?" Sandy asked.

"She said she had never done it – but, because my mother was listening, she didn't say if it was good or bad."

"Have you got any cognac?" Sandy remembered Lola had 'borrowed' our small bottle to make a pudding. There was an inch left in the bottle.

"Why don't we do half with and half without?" suggested Sandy.

"I asked my friend for some truffle to put in, but she didn't have any left. The truffle price is sky-high after the hot summer; the restaurants have taken them all." Asking a friend for 'black gold' to put in your *pâté de foie gras* might be stretching friendship too far, Sandy thought; like asking for her mother's pearls to decorate a cake.

They lit the charcoal fire on the terrace where they were going to cook, and Lola showed Sandy the ancient pressure cooker with its warped lid, repaired handles and suspect pressure gauge. Sandy could imagine the headline in the local paper, 'Two Peasant Women Die in Foie Gras Fiasco'.

They took out the trivet, filled the pot with water and set it to boil.

When the jars were cool, they were stuffed with the raw livers, topped with peppercorns and a bay leaf, and half of them had a teaspoon of brandy added. It looked impressive. 580 euros of anyone's money.

"If we stack them one on top of the other," Lola suggested, "we can do ten at the same time in that cooker." Sandy had a flashback twenty years to her grandmother bottling fruit. She had the impression that the water should not come above the top of the jars.

"Are you sure, Lola?" she asked. "There's no hurry. Five at a time would be fine."

"No, it will be O.K. I want to be finished before the kids get home from school."

The ten jars were stacked on the trivet and lowered into the cooker, the lid replaced and they waited for the pressure gauge to reach 100 before they started timing. With an hour and a half to kill, they made themselves some lunch and I joined them. It was quite a 'girls' lunch, with lots of talk about children and why we don't have any, mother-daughter angst and middle-age spread. I left them opening a bottle of white wine, and went back to my roof.

The one and a half hours came and went, along with half a bottle of wine.

"I think it must be time," said Lola ' Let's go and see!" Her eyes were sparkling. She was already spending her profits.

Gathering together cloths and rags to grab the handles, they lifted the cooker off the coals and onto the terrace. They had to wait for the pressure to subside, so they finished off the bottle of wine. In high spirits they lifted the lid. There was an oil slick, like a supertanker founded on rocks. A disaster. The water had a surface layer of emulsified yellow fat about six inches deep. Each jar as it came out was full of greasy water with a bay leaf floating in it, a gobbet of pink *pâté* sunk to the bottom, and the fatty yellow scum. All ruined. Profit margins had taken a dive.

Always anxious to dodge blame, usually by pining the offence on her clumsy, absent-minded third son – not around today luckily for him – Lola cursed her mother.

"I told you! This is my mother's fault. Cognac! She told me to use it, and she knew it would all go wrong. What a bitch!" The haste, the overloaded pressure cooker, the bottle of wine, the extra cooking time didn't come into it.

"Well, we still have six jars left," said Sandy 'What shall we do with them?'

"We will do it on the stove in the kitchen. Just in big pans of hot water. No pressure."

They set about rescuing the day, and when the pans were boiling away with their precious cargo, Lola had an brainwave.

"I know what we can do! There's wild boar and rabbit in the freezer. I'll defrost them in the microwave and we can make a mixed *pâté* out of them. It's not like *foie gras*, but it's good." Two rabbits and a rib-roast joint of wild boar appeared. Like all her husband's small game, the rabbits had gone into the freezer, uncleaned and unskinned. Heads, fur, guts and all. They would have to be prepared now, after defrosting. Lola and Sandy took the boar meat off the bones, while they were waiting.

"Have you ever prepared a rabbit before?" Lola asked.

"No. But I think I'm about to learn, aren't I?"

It wasn't difficult. The rabbit gave up its fur coat, like a dowager slipping out of her sable. Head and feet took a quick flick of the wrist. It was just the colon full of brown slime that Sandy had a problem with. She hoped 'Environmental Health' officers didn't choose now to do a spot check.....

All the meat off all the bones, Lola cut some fresh sage and thyme and mixed it up together with a slosh of red wine, and packed it into loaf tins to bake in the oven. Sandy added an artistic flourish of leftover bay leaves and peppercorns. It, too, was impressive; but it wasn't worth 580 euros.

"Leave the rest to me," said Lola. "The kids will be home soon, and I want to clear up. It's a pity it all went wrong. My mother – what a bitch. Wait, I should give you your money. Twenty euros was it?"

"Forty, Lola."

"Forty euros. What a waste!'

"Never mind." said Sandy "Next year – and don't forget we still have the six jars."

She came home tired and smelling of herbs and raw meat.

"How did it go?" I asked.

"Bit of a fiasco actually..."

When the last six *foie gras* came off the stove they didn't look very appetising. More than half the jar was fat, with a couple of inches of *pâté* underneath. It might be delicious, but we couldn't ask 30 euros each for them. Obviously the quality of the ingredients was everything, and supermarket special offers were not high quality. Sandy couldn't see herself force-feeding geese, so this might be her one and only home-made *pâté de foie gras*.

We decided to keep it for ourselves and to Hell with calories, cholesterol and our consciences.

A RITE OF PASSAGE

ONE OF OUR neighbours is a doctor. His door into the street is his garage door; the house is fifty yards away at the bottom of a walled garden. No bell. No entry system. You need his mobile number to tell him you've arrived, for him to come down and let you in. He guards his privacy, imagining, I suppose, that as a doctor in a village he would be 'on call' at all hours for split lips, cut knees and free roadside consultations about general aches and pains. We can't keep our distance. No such peace for us. Our gates are wrought iron, imposing but distinctly see-through. Except for one corner, the courtyard is no hiding place. We live in the 'garage'; a long vaulted room with tractor-sized wooden doors, next to the gates. Our lights are clearly visible, our voices clearly heard from the street. When we're in, we're in. If we hear our names being called, as they have been at all hours of the day and night, we have to answer. We can't play dead. One winter evening, moonless, dry and cold, we heard someone struggling to open our gates. The lock has been put on, and is now rusted on, upside down. You must turn the handle backwards. No-one remembers. There was frustration in the voice that called.

"Alistaaair!" We were quite snug by the woodstove, content with our own thoughts and listening with half an ear to Stan Getz.

"Alistaaaaaaair!" We exchanged a resigned look and got up to let Rico in. If we'd known what was about to unfold, we might have played possum, just that one time.

Rico was in a state of child-like excitement, as close as an adult gets to wetting himself.

"Come and see this! I can't believe it myself! Come on! Come on!" and he marched off towards his pride and joy, the Mercedes.

Lola was there waiting and she grabbed our arms, pinching our flesh."Alistair! Sandy! Wait till you see this! Unbelievable!" The night air was full of exclamation marks. With dramatic timing as good as Gielgud, Rico flung open the boot. In our wildest dreams or nightmares we might have imagined a new puppy, a one-stringed cello to go with the untuned piano, tools off the back of a lorry, some bartered hi-tech, must-have rubbish. We would never have expected to see what we saw. Nestled in the plush of a Mercedes boot – the usual place for golf clubs and Vuitton luggage – was a wild boar, a *sanglier*. Small but powerful, well muscled, all bristled fur, with small, mean eyes and eat-anything teeth.

I had a flashback to a scene from 'The Godfather'. A man wakes up in a soft white bed on a sunny morning to find his sheets soaked in blood. Throwing back the covers he finds the severed head of a horse.

This was no less incongruous, no less bizarre, though not as bloody. It was a road-kill. After heavy rains, *sanglier* prefer to walk along the road rather than get their feet muddy. They root around on the verge, backsides blocking the dark roads and write off several family saloons every winter. Adult males often get up and walk away from the confrontations, leaving a crumpled Citroën and a concussed driver to wonder what the hell happened. The *sanglier* in Rico's boot hadn't been so lucky. It was small, from this year's litter.

I asked Rico if the Mercedes had been damaged in the accident.

"No, I didn't tell you? WE didn't hit the *sanglier*. It was a Nimois. He was standing in the middle of the road waving his arms. Business suit and shiny shoes, so I stopped. An accident, he said. Car was damaged but never mind, he had insurance. No, it was awful because he thought he'd hit an animal. A dog maybe. He couldn't look, would I see if it was injured or dead?" Rico laughed.

"I knew it couldn't be a dog way out there – it had to be a *sanglier*. It was dead all right, but I made out it was badly injured. Wounded *sanglier* are dangerous, I told him. He'd better get away quickly before it came to, and I would take care of everything for him. He was so grateful, he gave me 20 euros for my trouble before he drove off. So, a *sanglier* without wasting a bullet or denting the car, and 20 euros in my pocket. Unbelievable!" The three younger children had come out to see what was happening.

A RITE OF PASSAGE

"Is it dead?" asked the seven-year-old.

"No, it's asleep," said his bigger brother, making loud pig grunts to frighten.

"Of course it's dead," said Lola "Wouldn't you be dead if a car hit you?" Emboldened, they leaned into the boot and prodded the body.

"You touch it, Alistair," said Djojo. I gently stroked the coarse hide, softly abrasive like a doormat.

"It's still warm," I said.

"The best time to butcher it," said Rico, and started barking orders at Gabby, to take the beast upstairs and wash down the plastic table. I looked at Sandy and we realised we were about to get blood on our hands.

I'm not mad about blood. As a scrum-half I'd seen enough of my own and other people's to last a lifetime. Sandy doesn't have the same hang-up. At sea she can have the head and entrails of a mackerel over the side of the boat and the fish in a frying pan before you can say 'breakfast', without batting an eyelid. My gaping wounds and jagged cuts are sorted in a matter-of-fact way. All good practice for what happened next.

"A drink," said Rico, "and then let's get on with it."

Pastis was being poured up on the neighbours' terrace. The look of glee in Lola's eyes is usually only seen on a woman's face after a successful day's shopping. She couldn't wait to start.

"Will you help me, Sandy?" she asked, watching for a reaction. To her credit, Sandy barely flinched. We understood that this was a test; would townies, English townies, be up to all the blood and guts?

"If you show me what to do," I heard Sandy reply. That's my girl! She was wearing an old work jumper and she rolled up the sleeves. Rico had honed the carbon steel knives to a razor edge and handed one each to her and Lola. Surrounded by the black night, the floodlit terrace was part operating theatre and part theatrical stage. I was happy to be in the chorus and not the leading man.

The girls were ready to go.

"Stop!" shouted Rico "Let's see who can guess how much it

EN GARD

weighs! A bottle of pastis says it's thirty kilos."

Gabby, the only other person to have lifted the beast, said, "Thirty-five kilos," and went to find the bathroom scales.

I split the difference. "Thirty- two and a half."

"One hundred and sixty," said Djojo who only weighs two sparrows himself.

"Fifty," said his sister, who only weighs a bit more.

Toni, at 20 years of age, all five o'clock shadow and brooding indifference, declined to join the fun.

"It weighs nothing. It is young."

Gabby climbed onto the scales, shouted his weight and then his father handed him the boar to hold.

"For God's sake keep still!" Rico shouted as the young man struggled to hold the animal long enough for him to read the total weight. The aggregate, minus Gabby, made the *sanglier* thirty-one kilos.

"But if Gabby took his shoes off, it would be thirty," said Rico with dubious logic and pastis maths.

"I win!"

Sweepstake over, Lola made the first long cut from throat to groin.

"If this was a male," she said "before we did anything, we would have to castrate it. If not the meat is tainted. Uneatable."

"Small mercies," Sandy whispered.

After the belly cut, the *sanglier* was rolled on one side and another incision made around the belly, towards the spine. One working towards the head, the other towards the tail, the girls separated the skin from the flesh. The body still had residual warmth and it steamed in the cold air. It was turned on its other side and they repeated the process, Sandy copying the mistress butcher. From time to time, in the best hospital 'soap' traditions, Lola called for a sip of water. One of us obliged, holding the glass, as now she was bloody past her wrists. I grabbed some kitchen-roll and mopped her brow.

The lesson continued up and down the sinewy legs; cut here, tear there, pull, pull harder! Most of the hide was gone, hairy squares and strips piled in a dustbin at the edge of the table. The

A RITE OF PASSAGE

hind trotters had some skin left on for hand-holds, otherwise only the head still had its fur. Crunch time, with glassy, sightless eyes and a pink, rubbery snout to deal with.

The small talk between Lola and Sandy had stopped. I knew that look on Sandy's face. A mixture of resolve and resignation that gets her through most things; disembowelling and decapitation would be a first though.

A bit of black humour might lighten the load. I put down my pastis glass and rushed over to the table.

"Stand back!" I shouted, "It's never too late!" and I started to pump the damp, sticky ribcage. There were cries of disgust.

"Alistair, stop!"

"No, not yet – we haven't tried everything," I replied, and moved to the pig's head, where I simulated mouth to mouth resuscitation and blew hard into the rubbery snout.

Horrified shrieks and squeals as I stood up, blood smeared on both cheeks, and I reached for my pastis. Had I really just given artificial respiration to a skinned corpse? Hannibal Lecter comes to town.

There was something primitive, almost forbidden about what was going on. I could imagine, and understand, the revulsion many people would feel. I had watched chimpanzees ruthlessly hunt and kill a colobus monkey. The brutality was shocking, as was the chimps' hysterical pleasure in ripping the monkey to pieces.

We weren't that bad. But there was a kind of feeding frenzy amongst us. Even the children pulling disgusted faces and pretending to be sick, could not tear themselves away. I was glad I was old enough to drink.

There is a God. Lola told Sandy well done, but she would do the rest; it was a bit complicated. "Watch me," she said, "and then next time..."

Honour satisfied, Sandy wiped her hands and happily joined the rest of the chorus line. Lola cut the ears and held them up on top of her head. She cut off the snout and held it over her nose, and making grunting noises chased the kids around the table. My sick performance had opened the floodgates.

EN GARD

Ears and snout in the bucket, Lola tugged the skin forward and peeled it off the head, with a sound like wet Velcro. There were just little hairy socks now. She asked Gabby and Djojo to hold the hind feet and pull the legs wide open.

Here we go, I thought, and looked at Sandy. She was standing right beside Lola, hands on hips, a study in concentration. It could have been a flower-arranging class or cake-icing lesson. The lungs, stomach and bowels went into the rubbish bin. The heart, liver and kidneys were handed to Rico to put straight in the freezer. Rico has a fondness for all those bits of animals no-one else in the family will touch; he salivates over tongues, trotters and brains. When he came back from the kitchen, he was armed with a cleaver. He was merrily drunk and shouldn't have had charge of a putty knife. The thought of him hacking off the boar's head and his own, in one swoop, seemed quite likely. Lola told him to be careful and he indignantly told her this was his job and he'd done it a hundred times before. He was a drunk with a cleaver. Nobody tried to stop him. As a group, we closed our eyes and stepped away from the table.

Thwack! Thwack! Thwack! "There! That's supper for Black," he cried and as we opened our eyes he held the dripping head over the balcony and dropped it into the yard for his dog.

I'd heard about war brutalising soldiers and civilians alike, until the horrors seemed normal. I hoped this evening wasn't going to have the same effect on us.

In a methodical way Lola now divided up the meat and bones into joints and roasts and barbecue portions. After an hour and a half the table was covered in a lot of blood and eight large chunks of *sanglier*. They looked exactly like the pork on any supermarket shelf; minus the sanitising polystyrene trays and cling film. It was over.

"*Eh, voilà,*" said Lola, rinsing herself, the table and the terrace with a hose. "We'll have a piece for your birthday, Alistair; Done on the spit. Roast potatoes in the juices." She licked her lips, the transition from dead animal to roast *sanglier* complete in her mind, even while her hands were still bloody.

It had been what you might call an education.

PIGS BY MOONLIGHT

THE CITROEN 2CV was the French equivalent of the Volkswagen Beetle; a cheap and cheerful way for families to join the motoring masses. But, besides visiting *grandmère* on Sundays, the car had a second curious utilitarian brief in rural France. It was famous for carrying a farmer, a pig, a bale of hay and a basket of eggs across a rutted field – without breaking the eggs.

These days 2CVs are collectors' cars. They are expensively restored, waxed and polished, and they are kept in garages not farmyards. On sunny weekends, they are brought out to wallow their way around long corners, and to fart their way along quiet lanes and across deserted village squares. I smile when I see them, not only because they remind me of brightly coloured hedgehogs, but because of a story that Rico told me.

We had a regular summons to 'come round for a glass' next door. On these evenings, pastis flowed freely and tongues loosened quickly. Lurid tales, childhood memories, triumphs, adversities and confessions tumbled out as the bottle emptied. Being broke followed by the high life had been the cycle of Rico and Lola's marriage. A year living in a luxury villa, and then a year collecting fag-ends off the street, to make roll-ups. During one of the hard times, Rico's brother arrived in his 2CV. He had three hungry children in tow, not a cent in his pockets. Rico and Lola had three children of their own. What little there was in the house would hardly stretch to four more mouths.

Out came the pastis. There were serious decisions to be made and some plans were put forward. Gypsy lateral thinking.

"The children must have food," said Brother, stating the obvious, "and we must have cigarettes and petrol." It had already been decided he would be staying, though God only knew where everyone would sleep.

"If I must work, so be it," he said. More pastis to cushion the

EN GARD

blow. "Where can I find work around here?"

"There's no work to be had," said Rico. "I've been searching for weeks."

To fill the larder for the winter, it looked like a more radical solution would have to be found. They attacked the bottle of pastis, hoping for inspiration. Just after midnight, with the first bottle nearly empty, Lola reluctantly suggested theft.

"I passed a farm the other day, and asked the man for a few vegetables. He said to me 'I have no cabbages for gypsies,' and he spat on the ground. May Papa forgive me, but I wouldn't think twice about taking some leeks and carrots from him. The farmhouse is a long way from the road. I don't think the dogs would hear us. We could fill the boot in no time. It would be for the kids..." This clearly required some thought, and the second bottle of pastis came out.

"For the children then," said Brother, "we'll do it!"

It turned out later, that when he said "we'll do it", what he meant was that Lola should do it.

And she did. Night after night she drove to the farm. By starlight, she filled the boot with potatoes, turnips, cabbages, carrots and leeks. She was careful to take only half a dozen from each row and at intervals, so that no big gaps appeared in the field. The cold store was filling up nicely. Then the farmer must have noticed the widening spaces as he weeded or watered. He lay in wait one night with two fierce dogs. It was a close thing, but Lola escaped without being bitten, losing a good shoe as she ran for her life.

For a couple of months they ate the vegetables. Mashed, grilled, roasted, fried or boiled, in soups, stews and pies. They weren't hungry but something was missing. Meat. A French plate without meat is like the French flag without red. Brother voiced it one evening. As he sadly regarded his supper, he said wistfully, "A little something to go with the vegetables would be nice..."

The next day he had an idea.

"This is what we do..." he announced. As was habitual, 'what we do', began with a brace of pastis. "To make our little courage big" was how Rico described it. Fortified, they set off into the night in Brother's 2CV, towards a pig farm he had spotted earlier

PIGS BY MOONLIGHT

that afternoon. They took the pastis with them, in case their courage wavered and to guard against the cold.

"I've already made a hole in the fence over here," said Brother. "Grab this bag and follow me. Watch out for the ravine."

"Ravine!?"

"Yes. Don't worry, it's not too deep – just there to keep people like us out."

Rico shushed him to a whisper. As they got closer, the pigs in and around the huts grew restless. They started milling about, surprisingly agile in spite of their bulk and short legs.

"Give me the bag," said Brother, and from it he took a hammer. He outlined the plan of action.

"We get hold of one of the pigs, wrestle it to the ground, then you get on top of it, hold it still and I'll hit it."

The truth was that it was 5,000 years since Rico's family had last hunted like this, and it showed. For nearly an hour they chased down the pig. The animal, the same size and shape as an armchair, could turn on a five cent piece. Rico and his brother on the other hand were having trouble just staying on their feet. The muck underfoot was treacherous. Over and over the pig slipped through their fingers and they fell flat on their faces. Covered in evil smelling slime, they cursed in whispers and wished they hadn't left the pastis in the car. Eventually the pig tired and they were more evenly matched. Although beast and hunters were slick and slippery with slurry, they at last had the pig on its side. Rico mounted it, and slithered around in an attempt to pin it down long enough for Brother to deliver the '*coup de grace*'. With a final squeal the pig's nightmare was over, and they were all covered in blood, as well as piss and shit.

"Back to the car with it," said Brother. "*Vite!*" But quick was not to come into it. One hundred kilos of dead-weight in a pig shape takes some shifting. More so when both it and the shifters are covered in muck and mud. The pastis had been good for their courage, but not their balance. It was pitch black and there was the ravine between them and safety. Roast pork was still a long way off.

They tried hoisting the animal onto their shoulders but that was hopeless. They tried dragging it along the ground, but even the pulling handles of tail and ears afforded no grip. They even tried kneeling behind the pig and pushing in tandem. They paused for a smoke and tasted the slime as well as smelling it.

"The door," said Rico, dropping his cigarette and thinking out loud.

"At a time like this you're thinking about doors?" said Brother.

"Yes, the door. We take the hut door off its hinges and put the pig on it. We use it like a sled." A good idea deserves good fortune. The door came off its hinges with no problem. The pig was easier to roll than to lift and soon they had it on the 'sled'.

"We can always roll him to the car if this doesn't work," said Brother, giggling.

The door did work, but magnified by the 2 a.m. quiet, it made an awful sucking noise in the mud.

"Slowly," cautioned Rico. "Very slowly."

He was right, any attempt at speed had the pig sliding uncontrollably off the door and threatening to crush them both. Gravity worked for them going down the ravine but against them as they strained and shouldered the contraption up the other side. They wished they could swap the pastis for some rope at this point. After an hour they arrived at the fence, and squeezed their prize through the hole. They manhandled it onto the back seat of the 2CV, with the aid of a few well-placed kicks.

"It's done," said Rico. "Let's go."

"Non," said Brother. "I've been thinking."

Rico stopped swigging pastis to listen.

"It's only November," Brother continued. "There are nine, sometimes more, at supper. We'll need more than one pig to see us through the winter."

Rico swallowed his mouthful of pastis. He shrugged.

"You're right. Besides, if we're caught, prison will be the same for one pig or two. Bring the door."

Back among the pigs, their technique somewhat refined, they soon had another prime specimen ready to dispatch. Brother said he didn't have the strength, or the stomach, for the hammer this time. It fell to Rico to do the dirty work.

PIGS BY MOONLIGHT

"Hold it very still," he told Brother 'I'm going to do it with one blow."

"*D'accord,*" said Brother, and Rico gathered himself for one powerful hit.

"Now!" he said.

At the last second, pig and brother moved. In a final desperate bid for freedom the animal squirmed. It was Brother's hand and not the pig's head that caught the blow, the full force of Rico's hammer. There was some loud squealing and not from the pig. Brother bit down hard on his sleeve to stifle his scream and filled his mouth with slurry.

"*Merde!*" hissed Rico, right on two counts. In fury he drove the hammer into the pig's brain.

With one usable hand and almost sick with pain from the other, Brother couldn't help Rico in the struggle to get the pig to the car. It took more than an hour this time. The ravine was like the Grand Canyon. Whether his strength and determination came from pastis, or the month of vitamin-rich vegetables, we don't know. With the last bit of adrenaline flowing, Rico bludgeoned the second pig into place on top of the first on the back seat. At this point he noticed that the universe had tilted slightly.

A 2CV may well carry a farmer, a pig, a bale of hay, and a basket of eggs, but a second pig is a pig too far. The rear bumper was touching the ground, while the front wheels were no longer in contact with it. It was more rocket on launch pad, than car on road.

"It will be all right," said Brother. "Besides, we have to go now – my hand..."

The two brothers climbed into the front seats, and the inclination reduced a few degrees. Rico started the car, turned on the headlights and realised the last of their problems. Instead of illuminating the road, the beams pointed far into the night sky and on into outer space.

"*Merde!*" Rico moaned. "With two stolen pigs, a brother with a broken hand, headlights pointing at the moon, shit everywhere and *gendarmes* behind every tree, we will have to drive home at 2 kilometres an hour! *Merde.*"

EN GARD

It was the start of a particularly lovely dawn when they pulled up outside the house. Rico hoped that Brother did not tire of pork and begin to fancy a bit of beef.

March 26th, 2004
Windswept and waiting for the swallows

Dearest Den,
We've had a miserable seven days of mistral. Suddenly it's clear how this wind can be used as a defence in murder trials. A plea of temporary insanity, brought on by a week of mistral. It's a Jack Russell of a wind, biting and worrying at you. Sinking its teeth in and not letting go; it wears you out. Straight off the Alps, down the Rhone valley and into our courtyard. When it stops blowing, every particle of dust has disappeared. There's a clarity of light and an intensity of colour; you feel you can see every oak leaf on faraway hills. It has me reaching for my paints and brushes. Almost makes the misery worthwhile. Victor Hugo defined Provence as 'anywhere affected by the mistral' – which we definitely are; but Provence, the department, is east of the Rhone – which we aren't. Around here, enterprising estate agents have invented a new area, Provence du Gard, and the magic word allows them to add a couple of noughts to their prices.

If it wasn't for the wind, I'd say this was the first day of Spring. Wild violets in the courtyard, wild iris by the roadside, and almond blossom everywhere. Yesterday we noticed clouds of insects in the air, which means that the swallows will arrive any day. Scotty has it marked in his diary as 10.10 a.m. on March 31st last year. He was on the chemical loo in the courtyard at the time and the sky went dark with birds. They arrive in waves; tsunamis of swallows. They winter in Africa and come back here every year to reclaim their nests. Before us, the house had been empty for ten years or more. We had nests in every room, on light fittings, coat racks, butchers' hooks and under rafters. They were little masterpieces, so we left them alone for the first year – we weren't using the rooms after all. But as soon as they had eggs or chicks, the birds became aggressive. Protective, I suppose. Dive-bombing if we went indoors for any reason. All Spitfire pilots in a former life. I began not to like them; fork-tailed, beady-eyed squatters. So, after they flew away in the

Autumn, we took down the nests in the house. This year the shutters will be closed, and they will have to start from scratch somewhere outside. They'll probably be furious. Though, with us around all the time, perhaps it's not such a desirable residence any more.

If it is Spring, then it's time to think about unpacking summer clothes. We seem to have been in three layers forever. Even in southern France, there is a uniform greyness about winter clothing; just a splash of red or purple on a scarf or gloves. Having worn nothing but black for years, I erupted into colour last summer. I've been missing it; making do with pink socks. To lift the gloom, I tried dyeing some jumpers bought at the local 'friperie' – but even in my hippie days, I wouldn't have been seen dead in the results. The 'frip', a second-hand clothes warehouse, is a mouth-watering selection of sequinned ball gowns and wedding dresses, fancy waistcoats and velvet bell-bottoms, home-knits and Dynasty suits; whatever takes your fancy. Many a happy hour...

Scotty is baking bread today, because the village shop closes on Fridays. The smell of warm wholemeal loaves is filling the garage. It's the indoor equivalent of fresh-mown grass, but edible. When we first came to France, finding a bread we both enjoyed was a problem. Scotty likes it doughy; I like it crusty, especially the crunchy ends. We started with baguettes, familiar and pronounceable. But they were too salt-glazed, and not enough substance – even for me. After lots of delicious experiments, we buy 'gros pain', if we can, from La Nougatine in Uzès. Discriminating between bakers as well as breads now. 'Gros pain' is good mopping-up bread, for sauces and salad drippings; but tearing it to shreds as you walk along the street is good too. We're not alone; less than half the bread makes it home in one piece. We can't help ourselves. My gran used to tell me to eat my crusts to make my hair curly. Here they tell little girls to eat the round ends of the bread to give them big breasts. For a couple of obvious reasons, I'm used as an example to prove this rule.

I'm hurrying to catch the post. Madame la factrice always likes an exchange of ideas and gardening hints along with the mail. Passion flowers are a worry for us both – to cut back or wait for fresh growth on old stems. We have a variety called 'Incense', exotic and almost sci-fi. It's a mistake to think it is delicate, just because it's beautiful. Look at lilies. Or roses. (Or me!?) Tough cookies. I think I'm going to cut back....

Your e-mails are full of news; they make me smile. But an old-fash-

WINDSWEPT AND WAITING FOR THE SWALLOWS

ioned letter would be a treat; something to rip open, like a bodice or a bag of crisps; something to keep.
   All love,
   Sandy and Scotty

FINDING OUR SPOT

WHEN WE LIVED in Brighton we had a 'local' that wasn't all that local. A stiff walk up a steep hill, which the dog enjoyed anyway. They brewed their own dark ale, and had guest beers with daft names that defied you to order them – "Two Dog's Bollocks, and a Stagger in the Dark, please." It was pretty basic; bare floorboards, brown paint and long pine tables which you usually shared, and so got into conversation with strangers. Conversations about sloops and bottle-necking, one-way systems and the arrogance of cats. It was a bit Thomas Hardy, though nobody ever came in trying to sell his wife.

There were seven other pubs between the house and the 'local' and occasionally, in a blizzard or a gale, we would duck into one of those instead. One of them had open fires and another had good food, but our allegiance never shifted and we always went back up the hill. We felt comfortable and at ease there, with the arthritic old sailors and hippie Golden Retriever, faded photos of steam engines and the single choice of salt and vinegar crisps. We'd found our spot.

Our local here would have to be a bar-café, the closest we could get to a pub. 'Closest' being not that close; a distant cousin at best. Our village had sold its last bar licence a long time ago for a handsome profit. The government isn't issuing any more. Once again, our local, when we found it, would be up a hill. And down. Not a walk, but a drive away.

Uzès is the nearby market town, with a long main street and an arched square full of plane trees. Along the street, around the square and in the alleyways that join them, are bar-cafés for every mood and pocket and manner of man.. We started in the 'top left-hand corner' and slowly over the months, worked our way down and around. Trying to find our spot.

The bar by the fountain is run by two brothers, a short square

FINDING OUR SPOT

boxer and a graceful heron, both with gelled hair and baggy shorts. Organised as ants, never writing down orders or missing a new face, we envied their energy and enjoyed their omelettes. Dogs bathed in the fountain and shook themselves dry, making rainbows. An old man, like Van Gogh's postman with a gauzy beard, took up one table, drawing endless pen and ink castles. Accordions like lungs of dinosaurs wheezed and a hat was passed round. We thought we'd found our place. But, in Summer, the fountain, the shade and the omelettes attracted too many visitors. They always found us a table for two, but we felt swamped and ousted from our spot.

At the other end of the main street was a working-man's café. All gleaming tiles and straight-backed chairs, floor regularly swept of fag-ends. No frills or fancy ideas, a nod to greet you and good hot *crème*. Aged Arabs met there, hands over their hearts, while their wives went market shopping. On Saturdays plates of oysters, six for three euros, were served at table. One young waiter, a case study in service without servility, came outside regularly to take an order and to check on his motorbike, running a sleeve over the chrome. He died skidding on some gravel last autumn. The bar closed for the funeral and the heart went out of the place. There was a sadness in the eyes of the patron and in the air, and we moved on.

The place next door was seriously attacked by some interior designers. Precious old film and bullfighting posters torn down and replaced by paintings of matchstick men. Nicotine-stained walls were painted burnt orange, cracked leather seats and Formica tables swapped for suede and chrome. Moving with the times. We preferred the old place and drifted away.

Coffee by coffee and *kir* by *kir* we went to most cafés, all through the seasons. We discounted the betting-shop bars and the *salons de thé*, full of men in wigs with champagne poodles. A tapas bar like Colonel Ghadaffi's tent lost us forever when, with half an hour to go before lunch, we wanted a drink and were refused. His glamorous neighbour, all bamboo, sarongs and potted palms, pressured us when our coffee lasted too long and tables were filling up. There is an unwritten rule here, that buying a drink buys you a table, for as long as you want it. It's polite to give it up at midday if you are not eating, otherwise it's yours. The rich pickings from summer visitors have changed that understanding in some places. Fair enough, business is business, but we go where we are welcome whatever the time of year and we hope that Uzès doesn't self-destruct with greed.

Nearly two years after the search began, we have our locals. Two spots we like for different reasons and we are not going to choose between them. One in the main street and one on the edge of the square, we call them The Mad Women and The Jazz Café.

The Mad Women are a mother and daughter. The mother looks like Walter Matthau with fluffy hennaed hair. She favours dark glasses, crushed velvet and silver bangles. The daughter is taller than most men, with eyebrows that lift independently in mock horror. She wears horn-rims and bell-bottoms and reads thick books. Both purse and pout a lot and have the lips for it. Theirs is an absent-minded and world-weary approach, with a lot of nostril-flaring and heavy sighs. Muttering, tutting and clucking and talking loudly to themselves, they seem pleasantly mad.

The café bumbles along around them. The backbone of customers are all-day tipplers, 'wine-before-nine' men and women. Later, lady friends lunch in large straw hats, alongside painters and decorators in speckled overalls. An art club meets there and the walls are covered in their work. Abstracts in black and white plaster, *papier-mâché* nudes and pointillist portraits. All of it optimistically for sale. The cook waves from the kitchen and blushes at compliments. It is a wry place, with cheap furniture and friendly dogs. We've had a lot of 'café moments' there; when ideas and solutions appear from mid-air. Rustling leaves overhead and murmuring conversations, bringing on a trance. Synapses start popping. It's a good spot.

The Jazz Café is really a wine bar. On the edge of the square, it looks onto the market, close to a mime artist and the garlic lady like a town crier, "*Ail! Ail! Ail! Profitez! Profitez!*" Chess players meet there and lose childishly, knocking over all the pieces and blaming the wind. They play all the music we would choose, Ella and Joe Cocker and lots of blues and jazz. Some we don't recognise, mellow and thought-provoking. You can have sun or shade, and inside it is cool and full of plants. A room full of blackboards chalked with philosophical asides; "Hell is other people" among them. The house *rosé* is a good way to round off the day, while ripping a *baguette* to pieces. You might have one or two philosophical asides of your own. A black Labrador from the shop next door pops over for a chat, and stresses and strains seep away. Another good spot.

The evening meal in France is still so important to the family that, at the time when pubs are just livening up, the bar-café is closing. The customers all go home to eat, and they don't come back later. Last orders, in our new locals, are 7.30pm. Earlier in winter. It took a while, but our clock slowly slipped back, and we come home to dinner too. We miss the beer sometimes, and even the walk up the hill, but not enough to go back.

THE ALIENS ARE COMING

"IS THERE anybody there?" politely asked through the gates.
No, I thought. Not when I'm this tired and this dirty.
Louder this time. "Is there anybody there?" As if I was obliged to be. A third time, and I knew it was not going to be ignored.
I came down from my ladder, dusty, bare chested and in ragged shorts.
"*Ah, bonjour, monsieur.*"
Two very serious women, wearing steel-rimmed glasses and no-nonsense haircuts, both with clipboards, and clearly pleased to have found someone's ear to bend. Teachers, I would have guessed. They extended clean, manicured hands to be shaken and then withdrew them, when they caught sight of my cement-encrusted paws. I tug at my right ear lobe when I'm agitated. As I did so, dried mortar fell from it. My hair and eyelashes were thick with dust. The two women kept their distance, but were not to be deterred.
They had a message and they plunged straight in. Well rehearsed, as one paused for breath, the other took over the diatribe. At breakneck pace, their voices rising in excitement, they took no account of my listening speed. I soon fell behind. They were very passionate, very anti-something. I guessed that from their clipboards, which held a petition; petitions are usually anti. The word 'alien' seemed to spring up often, but I did have mortar in my ears, and I was very tired. My resistance was low. I was going to sign, and just wished they'd hurry up, and leave me to my shower.
"*Alors?*" The duologue was finished and they were asking me for comment. I was aware that for five minutes or so, I had been preoccupied with their clash of pink lipstick and hennaed hair, and not listening at all. It reminded me of a fourth-form maths class where my mind had drifted from quadratic equations to ten-

nis. The master shouted "Scott?!" and I had to answer a question I hadn't even heard. I'm a more skilled bluffer at 50, than I was at 15.

"How many signatures do you have already?" I tried, keeping it non-committal. Pink Lipstick passed me the clipboard and said, when I had signed, they would have 101. I obliged and we wished each other a good evening. They went to try Alex's door, which, in fairness, I should have told them was actually his garage door.

"Well?" Sandy asked as I went inside. Somehow she always manages to be busy when religious cults and vote-gatherers come calling.

"Well what?" I said casually.
"Who were they?"
"Two women with a petition. I signed it."
"What sort of a petition?"
"It sounds ridiculous."
"Go on."
"A petition against the coming of the Aliens."
"Immigrants, you mean? Illegal immigrants?"
"They said 'Aliens.'"
"Where are they – the women, I mean, not the Aliens?"
"They were trying Alex next door."

Sandy stopped chopping onions and went outside to find the petitioners. The street was empty and so she returned to cross-examine me. All I could tell her was that I'd understood Aliens were coming, about ten or twelve of them, somewhere in the *garrigue* between here and Belvezet and that, bizarrely, the mayor didn't object. In fact, the women believed he was positively in favour of them. Part of his vision.

"I think we'll stay off the alcohol tonight," Sandy suggested. She had good reason. I don't usually talk that much rubbish, even when I'm exhausted.

Next day, in the usual bread-buying banter she found out the truth. Not Aliens, but Aeolians. My sum knowledge of Aeolians, were islands near Sicily, named after Aeolus, the Greek God of Wind. I thought there was an Aeolian harp too; a wind instrument, possibly. That was it.

"What's an Aeolian?" I asked coming down the ladder.

"It's what they call wind farms, or it's the name of the Company that builds them – or both," Sandy replied. "There's a project to put a dozen wind turbines in the *garrigue*. Between here and Belvezet. You got that bit right. Guess who's land they're going to use?"

"Go on."

"Who's got his finger in every pie around here?"

"Not Vertigo?" The previous owner of our house, whose favourite pastime was messing with people's heads while turning a quick buck. His last hare-brained scheme, was to have a dynamite depot near the village. "And next door think the mayor is in cahoots with him."

"Oh, come off it!"

"Anyway, no little green men, just great white windmills. There's going to be a village meeting on Saturday. We should go."

"Of course we'll go. Find out what the mayor's got to say."

Driving across France I'd seen a few wind farms on the big plains. A hundred windmills in a group stretching off for miles. It was part of the country's commitment to the Kyoto agreement, to reduce greenhouse gases. Their electricity went into the European grid, used by Italy and Portugal, rather than benefiting local towns and businesses. They weren't as brute ugly as nuclear power stations or hydroelectric dams, but they did look... alien.

To put a dozen windmills in the *garrigue* seemed like vandalism. It's one of Europe's wildernesses; an ocean of green scrub under an ocean of sky, home to wild boar and deer. Bird-life too; enormous buzzards, lazy on their thermals, surprising in their density, attesting to the vigour of the place. The only inroads Man has made until now, is to erect pylons, or to venture a few yards in, to bag a rabbit. The infrastructure and sub-stations to go with Aeolians would change it forever. Take something beautiful; take something unspoilt; take something that hasn't been fucked, and really fuck it. A nice touch of irony too, building near Belvezet, which means 'beautiful view'.

In a half-baked way we've tried, as a household, to cut down our greedy power needs for years. We lived without a car for a long time, saving all the big jobs for one weekend and hiring from Rent-a-Wreck. Squeezing in a run to a country pub. We lived in a large town and didn't feel deprived. In a French village with one bus a day, a car isn't a luxury, it's vital. We understand everything isn't black and white. Aeolians may be part of an energy solution, but while major consumers are doing pollution credit deals with the Third World, it only feels like fiddling while Rome goes up in smoke. If I could practise all that, in French, I'd say my bit at the village meeting.

Saturday came and the village hall was full. There was one conspicuous absence; the mayor. A spokesman from St Marcel, a village which, with their mayor's help, had stopped a similar project going ahead, opened the meeting. He explained the problems with the industrialisation of the countryside, the damage to tourism and property prices, the noise and the incongruity of the windmills. There were never jobs for local people, just speculation at their expense. We were shown a bad film which flickered like a Laurel and Hardy original. It felt as if it had been taken secretly without consent, ill-lit and badly focused. The soundtrack was only intelligible in the last five minutes. The audience was restless. If we were to mount a serious challenge to the project we'd have to get our act together. We would have to do better than this.

I didn't have the opportunity to speak. A heated argument started as the film ended. Lots of hysterical shouting about animal welfare and house prices. Opinions, informed and otherwise, about wind, solar and nuclear power. Not anarchy; local democracy in action.

Not everyone was anti. There was a cry for more hard facts – how much of the *garrigue* would be lost? The windmills would be visible from what distance? Exactly how much noise did they make? From how far away could they be heard? Were there studies of effects on wildlife? Who would profit locally? Were we going to take down the signs saying 'Tourisme Vert' and replace them with 'Tourisme Industriel'? I hoped our faith in French people-power wasn't going to be shaken. If asked, we would happily have joined a protest march carrying a banner; an English couple exercising their right to protect French wilderness. But no-one asked. Nothing was planned beyond this one meeting, and it hadn't been enlightening or inspiring.

The mayor's absence was noted. Politically, it seemed like a blunder, given all the gossip.

The two women with the petition were there. For the moment, they represent our active line of defence against the 'Aliens'. As I write, an anemometer is being erected to monitor wind strength. We hope the mistral doesn't blow.

The mayor has promised another 'official' village meeting, chaired by him, once the local elections are over. It should be interesting.

I don't know whether to quote Joni Mitchell, "it ain't Paradise; put up a parking lot", or to misquote François-René de Chateaubriand, "before Man there is wilderness, after Man there is desert."

POSTCRIPT:

A while later – a little too long later for our comfort – Dominique. our mayor, called for a referendum on the subject of the wind turbines. He was as good as his word, and not Machiavelli incarnate. In their wisdom, the folk voted overwhelmingly against the installation of the wind farm. It is a wonder to us that the villagers and their mayor enjoy this hands-on local democracy that works in practice.

At a boozy party, a member of New Labour in Brighton derided the existence of this grass roots politics, "Not necessary," he asserted, "when the electorate is more sophisticated." I suppose that he can't see the beauty of it and is unaware of the danger of dismissing it.

For our part we are grateful for our mayor and his part in upholding freedoms. He is the steward of something very precious.

SANDY'S SIXTY CLOVES OF GARLIC WITH CHICKEN

OUR SENSES ARE threads that join us to our past. Not only *déjà vu*, but also *déjà* heard and smelt, touched and tasted.

My old geography teacher seems to be selling kebabs in the market; the lavender stall has me leaning into my mother's linen chest. A tobacco-stained beard; a magpie laugh; too tart *citron pressé*; a smiling dog stopping for a pat; McCartney's 'Long and winding road', cross-stitching and weaving you back and forth.

For me, 'already seen' is the least powerful thread; no more than a frozen frame. Taste and smell are the most evocative time-machines.

I was a slow starter with food – well past my first, and last, cigarette before smoked salmon or avocado passed my lips. Garlic even later. In a plate of pasta Alfredo in a Sicilian kitchen, cooked by the man who came to water the garden, and who gave me a handful of apricots for dessert. I can feel the warm hairy fruit, hear him singing in dialect and see his perfectly-ironed shirt. For a few seconds when I crush a clove of garlic, I am there – twenty-one again and I still have a waist.

This recipe takes a lot of time preparing the garlic; let your memories roll.

You will need – a chicken, corn-fed and weighing 3 to 4 lbs; sixty cloves of garlic, give or take; 6 tablespoons of olive oil, a good one but it need not be your best; a stick of celery; sprigs of parsley, sage, rosemary and thyme, and a bay leaf; salt and pepper.

A chicken 'brick', which cooks the chicken in its own juices – Habitat used to sell them in the 1970s, but they may have fallen out of favour. It must be a pot with a lid anyway.

Pre-heat the oven Gas 5/375°F/190°C.

Season the inside of the chicken and place the thyme there.

Put all the other herbs, celery and the separated, but unpeeled cloves of garlic, in the 'brick' with the oil. Toss the chicken in the mix until it is drenched in oil.

Replace the lid and cook for 1 hour 30 minutes.

Don't deprive your guests of the blast of garlicky herbs as you lift the lid – make sure you do it at the table.

When you eat, squash the cloves with a fork to break the skins, and scrape out the sweet sticky flesh.

Sixty cloves isn't written in stone. It can be twenty or one hundred. Up to you; how much pleasure can you take?

THE PARTY TO END ALL PARTIES

MARCH 27TH IS Lola's birthday. Party time. This year she had two other good reasons to put on her dancing shoes. She had spent three days in hospital and had the all clear on another cancer scare. She was still not firing on all cylinders – but sixty per cent of Lola is usually more than enough. During the year, by happenstance, her two eldest sons had fallen head over heels in love with two gypsy girls, and having gone through the ritual 'kidnapping' and 'deflowering', the couples were now betrothed.

Every gypsy knows that a double marriage means one of the couples leave with both lots of good luck. But somewhere in Lola's costing process for the weddings, pragmatism got the better of superstition. What rubbish that one couple may benefit at the cost of the other! They would each have to make their own luck. The weddings would be on April 10th, at the same place and at the same time. It would save a fortune.

It meant that Lola was a bit pressed for time to bring the extending families together before the weddings. A chance to stamp her authority on affairs, to weigh up the future in-laws and establish a power base. She might be gaining two 'daughters', but she had no intention of losing two sons. It would be best done on her home territory. If she doubled up the usefulness of her party, the in-laws could meet for the first time at her house on March 27th.

Lola came round to explain the new significance of the celebrations, to show Sandy her party frock and to establish, for the umpteenth time, that we would be there. I could not see the outfit before the party – as it might bring bad luck. Some superstitions, that don't cost too much, linger on. As it turned out, Lola could well be right, and I must have caught a glimpse of the dress in its plastic bag, for there was soon to be bad luck in abundance. I don't suppose it helps that March 27th falls in the thirteenth week of the year.

EN GARD

Sandy spent Saturday in front of a PC in the Internet Café Jourdan, in Uzès. I waited for her, writing longhand on paper with a proper pen, taking up space at busy cafés. The patrons didn't seem to mind at all. They sidled up to me, to catch a glimpse of the writing, going away disappointed that it was English. The day's work meant that we arrived home later than we had planned. We were both drained by a day of concentration and would have liked to go to bed; falling asleep to the World Service. No chance. We thought we could rinse our faces and not be too late for Lola's big night, and we might slip away early. A couple from England, house-hunting in a camping van, as we had done, were waiting for us in the village. They had called to say their goodbyes – they were heading off to Spain to find their dream home. We invited them to stay over and come to the party with us.

"It's a gypsy party," I said, "and you won't easily forget it!" They declined the offer, shared a last pastis and headed for sangria.

It was eight-thirty when we slipped next door, and the party was in full swing. Start early and finish late, that's the rule around here. Formal introductions weren't easy against the music and the babble. We made ourselves known, as best we could, to unfamiliar faces; kissed and shook the hands of everyone else. Perhaps because we had worked too long and were weary, we couldn't pick up the party mood. We felt as distant from it, as the in-laws seemed from each other. It was all a bit stiff and forced. We hoped it would liven up later, for Lola's sake. Be careful what you wish for – the gods sometimes grant it.

Lola did her very best to help the party along. Her new dress was black and red velvet, and as tight as a facelift. She led the dancing, and as usual, her dancing was coital. The in-laws, bewildered and then horrified, stiffened their backs visibly in their chairs, and their feet didn't tap out a single beat. Lola couldn't have given a damn.

Rico and Lola's parties never want for alcohol, but Sandy and I just could not raise our game, and for the first time in that kitchen I drank moderately. Mostly, we decided, we wanted to eat, and sleep soon after.

THE PARTY TO END ALL PARTIES

The rooms given over to the party were smoky enough, and I went outside to have my pipe. On the terrace, a woman was being violently sick into a bucket. I recognised her as one of the future mothers-in-law and asked her if she needed anything. That was my first mistake. I smoked, admired the moon, found Venus as bright as ever and went back to the party. I spent the time with Sandy, and with Pedro and Michelle, our over-the-road neighbours. We talked of Portugal and grilled sardines, and we 'stole' some slices of quiche from under the tablecloth covering the buffet. Then I went for my second smoke on the terrace.

Madame still had her head in the bucket of vomit. A daughter was sitting beside her with a consoling arm around her shoulders. Without asking this time, I fetched a glass of water, a damp flannel and a tube of toothpaste and gave them to the daughter. That was my second mistake. I smoked, then went back inside, ravenous by now. I had no inkling of the danger I was in.

The tablecloth was perfectly white and beautifully embroidered. It was handled as reverently as the Turin Shroud, as it came off the table and Gabby was sent to put it back in its drawer until the next very special occasion. There was a gravitational heave towards the food. Sandy and I helped ourselves, and sidestepped the crush. Toni's prospective father-in-law, Pascal, got his food, without a fuss. He is, after all a man six feet six inches tall and weighing in at 17 stones. Sandy ate in his company for 15 minutes, and he interrogated her about England and the English. She had no inkling of the danger I was in, either.

The food did nothing to revive our party spirits, and we decided to leave. Politeness required we excuse ourselves to our hosts, to thank them and wish them a *'bonne fête'*. While we were doing the rounds, I saw Madame sitting next to her husband, Pascal, her head no longer in the bucket.

"Are you feeling better, Madame?" I asked. It was a diplomatic calamity and my third mistake.

We set out for home and bed. On the terrace I remembered the keys were on the kitchen dresser. Sandy went back to hunt for them and she paused to bid Pedro and Michelle goodnight. I remember wondering what was taking so long. I crossed my arms in front of my chest, my legs at the ankle, leant on the railings and watched the door for her to reappear. Sandy was not the first to come through the door. It was Pascal. He didn't speak. He crossed the terrace and my line of vision from right to left. I still had no idea of the danger I was in.

Lola's nephew, the son of her late sister, who is fond of Sandy because she gives cut flowers to Lola's 'house-shrine' to his mother, was playing on the terrace with a friend. He saw what happened next and told me about it later that week.. Pascal had waited until he was sure I was looking away from him and then he had launched a savage attack. He had taken three long strides quickly and fisted me hard in the face. Completely unprepared, I had buckled at the knees, but didn't fall, and he fisted me again. Between the blows, he bellowed that I had tried to seduce his wife. The little boys had screamed in fear, and run indoors shouting that there was a fight and it involved Alistair.

I have a hazy recollection of wanting to get to the steps and away. Once there I think someone guided me gently down them, and to safety. In my ringing ears there was a lot of shouting on the terrace but I could make no sense of it. Down in the street my head started to clear and an unholy rage filled me. Inside Lola's house, Sandy had heard that I was in a fight.

"Alistair?! Alistair?! In a fight?!" she asked everyone on her way to the terrace. "It's not possible!" Sandy knows that my last fist-shaking had been on a rugby field 36 years ago. She found me outside our gates, with Rico and Djimmy trying to smooth things out, using all the wrong tactics.

"Alistair – *ce n'est pas grave*... it's nothing to us; we don't care – everything's O.K." Djimmy was saying.

"It bloody well is '*grave*'!" I shouted, pulling myself out of their restraining arms. "And it's me that decides if it's O.K or not – not you. Now leave me alone."

Sandy told Rico that it might be best to leave things be for tonight, and we could sort it out tomorrow. She said Pascal had a mentality very different from ours and perhaps he was drunk, but that was no excuse to behave like an animal.

"Please go back to the party, and we'll talk about it in the morning," she said and closed the gates.

In the garage I was full of anger and there was nowhere for it to go. Sandy tried to find out exactly what had happened. Pascal thought I fancied his wife and in some kind of jealous red mist, had belted me, I told her. Not by squaring-up, man to man, but by waiting until I wasn't looking and coming at me from one side.

"Why would he think you fancied her?" Sandy asked "You didn't dance with her. You didn't even dance with me – you danced with Jean-Claud for two minutes and that's all."

"God knows! She had her head in a bucket of vomit all night. All I did was get her a glass of water and a facecloth. That'll teach me." Then we had a stream of visitors at the gate. All of them were in tears. Rico and Djimmy came back and Sandy went out to see them. They wanted repair; for everything to go on as if nothing had happened. Sandy said again that we should leave things until the next morning. Djimmy came back with Lola, who was distraught and begging to talk to me. I wasn't talking to anyone. Gabby came on his own, repeating over and over that his family were not to blame and for us not to think badly of them. Then Toni arrived; it was Pascal's daughter he was to marry. Sandy insisted that I should talk to him myself.

"I love you like an uncle, Alistair. *Je suis desolé.*" "*Desolé*" is as sorry as you can be; to an English ear it conjures up desolation. I told him how angry I was, but not with him. At that point Pascal turned up, wanting forgiveness. It was the last thing on earth I could give him, and Toni had the sense to take him away.

While I was pacing out my rage in the garage, back in her kitchen Lola told Pascal that he would never be welcome in her home again. That he had no respect for her or her family or friends. She told him that for 18 months of her illness, there were only two people looking in on her – Sandy and Alistair. What he had done was to attack her 'brother'.

The party was over. We sat in the garage hearing car door after car door slam as people left. Jean-Claud is Lola's brother-in-law. He is a gentle and thoughtful soul. He was the last to leave because he had comforted Lola. As he passed the garage I heard him call.

EN GARD

"Good night, Alistair."

His son echoed him. It was just above a whimper.

For three nights and four days I chose a self-imposed exile in the garage. I padlocked the gates. It felt like a powerful symbolic gesture and I enjoyed that. I heard later that people passing by hated to see the chain, but I wanted no contact with the world apart from Sandy. Sandy suffered; sharing the garage with a fury that would not subside, and a man preoccupied with endless sadistic, murderous and revengeful thoughts. Especially during the small hours. I was horrid and I could not stop myself. Gabby brought me out of it. I had crossed the road to fetch something from the car.

"Alistair, *ça va*?"

"*IM-PECC-ABLE*," I bellowed. I knew it would punish him.

Later the chain was still unfastened. Gabby is young and uncomplicated. He's resilient and gutsy, too. He walked through the gates, into the garage and hugged me. It lanced the boil at once.

"My mother has cried every day since Saturday. My father has telephoned every day from work to ask if anyone has spoken with you or seen you. It has been hard for us."

"For me too, Gabby, it has been hard. Perhaps harder for me than for you, huh?"

Gabby was 14 at the time. Better than Henry Kissinger. He paused just long enough and said, "Alistair, please come round. Have a drink and talk to my parents."

"I'm not ready for that, Gabby. I'll do it tomorrow."

"*D'accord*. Tomorrow, then."

As Gabby walked out of the gates, Rico and Lola arrived home from the supermarket.

"Gabby, have you just spoken with Alistair?" Rico asked.

"Yes, papa. He's coming for a drink tomorrow."

"Oh no, he's not," said Rico. "We'll do it now"

We did drink and we talked till late. I spoke about my anger, hurt and humiliation. Of my disbelief that I could be attacked in their home. I told about my damaged face, and that I thought Pascal, their new family member was a sick and dangerous man.

THE PARTY TO END ALL PARTIES

Especially if he thought that anyone could find his wife attractive while she stank of vomit, the stuff matted in her hair and dribbled down her clothing. Lola and Rico said that they were deeply sorry and ashamed, and that Pascal had been ordered out of their house, never to return. They also told me that they would not be going to their sons' double wedding. Lola said that if she could not invite cherished friends to a family celebration for fear of their safety, then she would not go herself. She had made a choice. New family or established friends? It was easy, she said – friends don't come cheap, fools do.

Sandy and I were horrified. We had no need to be seen to gain a victory over the fool. We had no wish for Djimmy and Toni to be married without their parents present. We asked them to reconsider, and then we all got drunk.

They did reconsider. On Saturday evening, just seven days after the attack, they told us they had called off the wedding on April 10th. The two sons would stay betrothed, but their marriages were postponed indefinitely. Toni left home and went to live with his new family. I hope he'll be happy there; but I suspect otherwise.

As his mother explains, "They're gypsies, Alistair. But they are not Manouch gypsies. They are Beringues. They are not the same. They are not civilised like us."

In the days that followed the attack, we had to visit Uzès. The tourists, like the swallows, had not yet arrived in huge numbers; Uzès still felt winter-small and calm. I wanted to walk the streets for the pleasure of it. I pulled into a car park in a field in the centre of town. An attendant waved me towards him to pay. Another of Lola's nephews, who worked there, told him, "Non. He's for me." Through the car window he looked carefully at my bruised face.

"*Je suis desolé*, Alistair. Please excuse us." He is a young gypsy man. Very proud. The parking was free. And still is.

Jean-Claud hailed me from a café where he and his son were taking tea.

"It's a disgrace," he said, "I hope you're O.K." A third gypsy called to me from a bar, "Alistair, join me for a glass!" I might have seen him once before. The gypsies in France have a rough time.

EN GARD

They experience racism and are held in contempt. It takes a fool of a man two seconds of gratuitous violence to reinforce that. However, if Pascal takes gypsies one step backwards, he should know that others work long and hard to move them two steps forwards. The young gypsy men know about the attack on a man who did not bring prejudice and contempt to them, and they share a group shame. I did not milk it, but it salved my hurt. It also made me very proud of them.

THE END OF THE BEGINNING

IN THE FIRST week of April, the high pressure system must have been delayed somewhere. Morning after morning, I craved the blue-blue skies, and had to make do with grumpy grey.

I moaned to Sandy and she said, 'We can always sell up and move somewhere else."

"Non," I replied. "*Pour le premier fois dans ma vie*, I don't want to live somewhere else." The sentence was half French and half English. It sounded about right.

SKETCH PLAN OF THE HOUSE

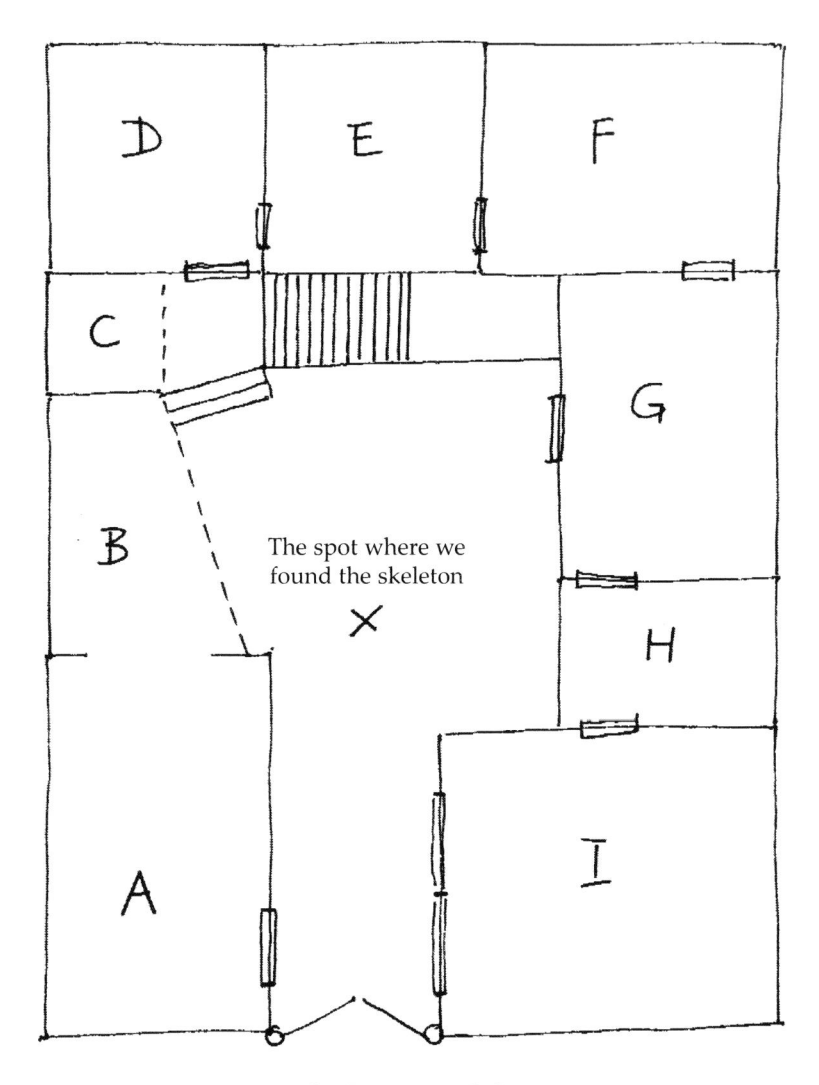

The spot where we found the skeleton

GROUND FLOOR
A - Sandy's studio, B - Summer dining room, C - Summer kitchen, D - Kitchen/dining room, E - Sitting room, F - Walk-in pantry/cold store, G - Use not decided yet, H - Bathroom, I - 'Garage' (our living space during the work).

SKETCH PLAN OF THE HOUSE

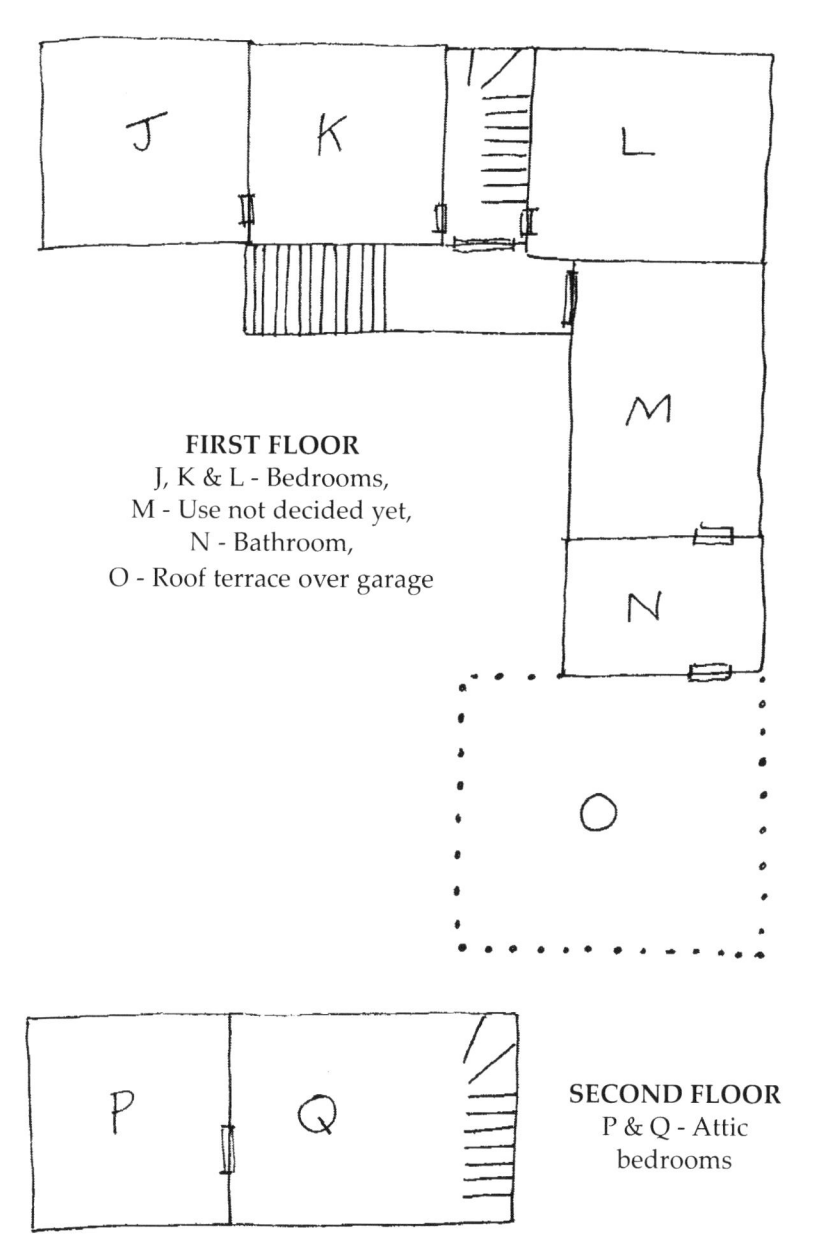

FIRST FLOOR
J, K & L - Bedrooms,
M - Use not decided yet,
N - Bathroom,
O - Roof terrace over garage

SECOND FLOOR
P & Q - Attic bedrooms

Some of the French-themed books published by the Léonie Press:

A BULL BY THE BACK DOOR
by ANNE LOADER
ISBN 1 901253 06 6   £8.99

THE DUCK WITH A DIRTY LAUGH by ANNE LOADER
ISBN 1 901253 0 90   £8.99

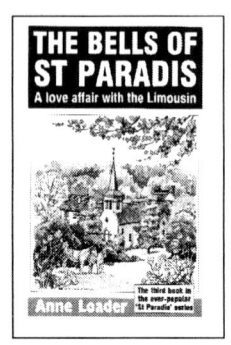

THE BELLS OF ST PARADIS
by ANNE LOADER
ISBN 1 901253 26 0   £9.99

ONLY FOOLS DRINK WATER
by GEOFFREY MORRIS
ISBN 1 901253 10 4   £8.99

OU EST LE 'PING'?
by GRACE McKEE
ISBN 1 901253 11 2   £7.99

THE HIDDEN TRIANGLE
by VALERIE THOMPSON
ISBN 1 901253 32 5   £8.99

19 - CUISINE DU TERROIR CORRÉZIENNE
by MALCIOLM ALDER-SMITH
ISBN 1 901253 43 0   £11.99

BANANAS IN BORDEAUX
LOUISE FRANKLIN CASTANET
ISBN 1 901253 29 5   £10.99

POLLY TAKES THE SCENIC ROUTE by GAY PYPER
ISBN 1 901253 33 3   £8.99

For more details visit our website: www.leoniepress.com